BARCODE KILLERS

THE SLIPKNOT STORY IN WORDS AND PICTURES

FIRST PUBLISHED IN GREAT BRITAIN IN 2001 BY CHROME DREAMS.

P.O. BOX 230
NEW MALDEN
SURREY
KT3 6YY
UK

A CATALOGUE RECORD FOR THIS BOOK IS AVAILABLE FROM THE BRITISH LIBRARY.

TEXT BY MARK CRAMPTON.
ADDITIONAL MATERIAL BY ROB JOHNSTONE AND JAMES TOMALIN.
SCRIPT READING BY SYLWIA LUBKOWSKA.
DESIGN BY JON STOREY AND DAVID BALFOUR.
SPECIAL THANKS TO MIKE LAWYER AT SR AUDIO, DES MOINES.

PRINTED AND BOUND IN THE UK.

BARCODE KILLERS

the slipknot story
in words and pictures

www.chromedreams.co.uk

contents

The early days of the Des Moines' Destructors. Bored and uninspired, the future Slipknotters find a welcome saviour in heavy metal and prepare to unleash a multi-legged metal-monster onto an unsuspecting local music scene.

With an impressive live show and growing local adulation, the band enter the recording studio to get their new sound down on tape. As costs spiral out of control, the band release *Mate. Feed. Kill. Repeat.*, a take-away slice of Slipknot for home consumption.

Slipknot beat the cream of the local Des Moines scene to win the prestigious Battle of the Bands competition. With old members leaving and new ones arriving, the recently Masked Marauders tighten the team and play their biggest gig to date.

With the sic-ness spreading, Slipknot sign to Roadrunner Records. Under the direction of nu-metal producer Ross Robinson, the band get down to recording their major label debut.

The perfect compliment to Slipknot's live shows, the band's debut album rockets up the music charts. In the midst of controversy and a final line-up change, the band discover that things will never be the same again.

Introduction

The State of Iowa in the United States is not best known for being the centre of musical advancement. In fact, this ultra-conservative 'bible-belt' area is far more famous to outsiders for its pig and corn industries rather than its music. So the backwater town of Des Moines wouldn't seem the ideal location to spawn the next stage in the evolution of modern heavy metal. Would it? Well, it's time to rewrite the history books and think again, because against all the odds it's done just that.

Slithering out of the stultifying Mid-West confines of Des Moines, a band going by the strange name of Slipknot, who began as the heart and soul of the town's new, brutally heavy underground scene, have officially started their earthly rampage on Planet Rock. From out of this 'nowhere' zone, a rampant beast has come crashing down upon the music world, totally dedicated to confronting everything we've heard before. Having steadily grown from six pieces to nine since their inception in the mid-1990s, Slipknot are guaranteed to give you something of a major brain scramble soundwise. If that's what you're looking for from your music, then this is the band for you. What they present best is a radical, no-holds-barred picture, reflecting the harshness and ugliness of commercialism today. Dressed in matching jump-suits, each individually numbered, the members of Slipknot are purveyors of an over-the-top metallic mayhemic madness that has never been tapped in the metal community before.

Having nine members in a band may sound completely over the top to many modern rock fans. However, there's more to Slipknot than meets the eye (or the ear for that matter). Stuck for many years in the creative wastes of nowhere, with nothing but industrial underground and hard-core rap to listen to, Slipknot have managed to come up with an original, yet brutally precise, primal style of metal. And as huge as they sound on stage and on record, they look even sicker draped in their demented masks, ranging from those of circus clowns to toxic waste specialists. Imagine if Charles Manson had grown up on the new jack-metal scene populated by bands such as Korn, The Deftones and System Of A Down and that he had an appreciation for speed-metal heavyweights, Slayer. Instead of committing hideous crimes, he'd probably have been a founding member of Slipknot. So belt up tight and prepare to hop on the shuttle that takes lunacy to bizarre new levels. Welcome to the world's most insane band.

Chapter 1.

Collective Hate

The story of Slipknot is inexorably linked with the city of Des Moines, where all the future members spent their formative years. Like suburban towns the world over, it was a fine place to live until adolescence came calling and almost overnight it simply became the capital of boredom. Although school amply filled their days, leisure time for most teenagers in town revolved around the Mall, McDonalds and the ice rink. Sound familiar? For the rebelling future Slipknotters and their gangs, none of these seemed very appealing. Instead, they took to hanging out at the local Woodland Cemetery. To preserve appearances, they would get their parents to drop them off at the skating rink, but would then duck out the back to spend the evening in the graveyard. Once among the graves, they would get drunk on stolen, begged or borrowed booze. In fact, they drunk so much that they would sometimes stoop to fantasising about digging up the graves and finding a skull to drink from. With so little to do, boredom quickly led to vandalism and mindless destruction of the fabric and infrastructure of the town centre. Later, when they got driving licences, they found a whole new bag of tricks to play with. A popular pastime was driving around knocking over traffic signs and shouting obscenities out of the car windows at passers by.

In the midst of this tedium, however, the youngsters found their saving grace in the form of heavy metal. Listening to bands such as Slayer and Black Sabbath gave them a new release for their feelings, lifting the stultifying atmosphere and providing them with a vision of something real beyond the town boundaries. As teenagers, many of the future Slipknotters were inspired enough by the metal they heard to start playing instruments themselves. They soon formed high-school metal bands to replicate the music of their idols, channelling the hate and violence they once directed at the town into their music making. Playing to school friends, however, was the only way to get their music heard as at this time there was a complete lack of suitable venues for bands to play. In addition, the local shops were not big on stocks of metal albums and the future members of Slipknot had a hard time getting hold of the music they so badly needed.

Although the off-the-beaten-track location of Des Moines meant that many of the big rock acts would not include it on their tour itineraries, one rare local performance did have an enormous effect on the youngsters. On the 20th of January 1982, the Godfather of metal, Ozzy Osbourne, descended on Des Moines for a show. During the gig a fan threw a live bat on stage and Ozzy, thinking it was made of rubber, bit its head off. Needless to say, he was banned from ever performing in Des Moines again. The future Slipknot members were too young at the time to attend the gig, but grew up hearing about this legendary moment from older fans in town. Although they were robbed of seeing their hero in the flesh, the story made a big impression on them. In fact, even to this day they believe that this event left a little bit of Ozzy in all of them.

The primary origins of Slipknot came about due to the friendship of two future members, Anders Colsefni and Shawn Crahan. They had met via the local music scene through playing in their respective high-school metal bands, VeXX and Heads On The Wall. While attending each other's gigs they had discovered that they were both into the role-playing game Rage, a more sinister version of Dungeons and Dragons. They began to meet on a regular basis at Crahan's parents' house and played out their fantasies for hours on end. In 1993, they started writing songs together and discussed forming a band with another friend, Paul Gray, who had been with Anders in VeXX. Despite their good intentions however, Shawn found himself too busy and the plans came to nothing.

Later though, in 1995, Anders was helping Shawn in his garage with some welding work and they again started discussing the possibility of forming a new band. At this time both were playing in other groups but felt that they weren't really making any headway. They had both become seriously disillusioned and frustrated with the small local music scene that didn't really cater for metal. Whenever they got the chance to play a gig they faced constant degradation, abuse and a complete lack of respect for what they were trying to achieve. To counter this negativity they now wanted to do something that was radically different, something that had never been done before. They wanted to rock the local scene to its core and shake it so hard that audiences would be forced to sit up and take notice. Shawn sensed that young people in town were ready for a complete show, rather than just a bunch of guys playing with a standard band line-up. He had a vision of a mega-group that didn't slavishly follow current musical trends and went all out playing what they, and they alone, wanted. He decided to accelerate the percussive side of the music, paring the group back to basics, with three drummers spaced across the stage to create a real hardcore back line. With this vision, Slipknot was born.

With their master-plan foremost in their minds, Anders and Shawn set about filling the ranks of the band with other disaffected musicians in town. Given the small size of Des Moines, the music scene was somewhat incestuous and contained a hard core of different metal and grindcore bands that had opened for each other at various times, shuffling members back and forth as new groups formed and older ones folded. At this time it seemed that many other musicians were feeling the same way about their bands as Shawn and Anders. They could therefore pick the cream of the crop. Anders approached Paul Gray again to play bass. As well as playing in Anders' old high-school bands, he had more recently played with him in the group Body Pit which was now hitting the skids. With Anders on vocals and Paul on bass, Shawn fell naturally into the role of drummer. Within a few weeks though, Shawn decided that he wanted to concentrate on percussion and the search went out for a replacement. While Paul had been in Body Pit, he had also played in a band called Anal Blast with the town's top drummer Joey Jordison. Joey was impressed by the direction the new band was hoping to take and was swiftly recruited. A month later they decided it was time to add a guitarist to the mix and called in an old friend Josh Brainard. He had previously been in VeXX with Anders and Paul and had also played guitar with Joey in the band Modifidious. He started adding noise and wah-wah pedal work over the top of the core bass and drums that the original members had put together. The addition of another Body Pit member, guitarist Donnie Steele, completed the line-up for the time being and the band was officially formed in September 1995.

The group then started regular rehearsals in the basement of Shawn's parent's house. They quickly made the space their own by sound-proofing the walls with scraps of carpet that they salvaged from a pet-grooming centre. Although this made the room more usable for rehearsing, it did have a serious drawback as animal urine had soaked into the carpet over the years and subsequently made the cellar stink. But despite the smell and the small size of the room, which left the band crammed on top of each other, they got down to working on the Slipknot sound. From these earliest sessions they specifically set out to experiment with a whole range of different musical styles, trying to escape from the usual polished three chord tricks of so many other bands. Due to the shared metal heritage of each and every member, the as yet unnamed Slipknot was always going to be based around hard, biting metal riffs. However, outside this core area each member brought in a host of different musical tastes and influences that were added to the melting pot. Staying true to their intention of playing what they wanted, they spiced the music with a highly unusual and diverse range of styles from funk to disco and jazz to rap.

After a couple of months rehearsing the band was keen to try out their new material on a live audience. Happily, a local promoter was casting around for a band to play at a local charity gig he was organising. As a result, in late November 1995, the group took to the stage at the Crobar Club in Des Moines. Forced to come up with a name at short notice, they settled on the rather bland title Meld. This was suggested by Josh who thought it amply reflected the band's experimentation with different musical styles. They kept this name for a month before changing it to the short lived PygSystem after which they finally agreed on Slipknot. This new moniker was taken from the title of a song that they always opened

with at gigs and given it was catchy and easy to remember, it stuck. It also suited the music they played and conjured up a specific image for the band of someone tied to a stake with evil all around. They felt this was like their music, trapping listeners, holding them down so that they couldn't escape from the relentless blast.

Fresh from their first gig, the band were now keen to perform as much as possible, but found it hard to get bookings. Apart from the fact that there were so few venues in town, they came up against the old apathy that had dogged them for years. The only regular gig that they could pick up was at the Safari Club, a local reggae bar in a seedy part of town. This was set up for cover bands, but on Thursday nights the owner turned it over to Slipknot for the evening. At first, the band had trouble getting a crowd into the venue, so they decided to blanket flypost the

town. With mountains of Slipknot flyers appearing in just about every public place, they were soon packing the venue to the gills. Unfortunately, the posting of several thousand Slipknot flyers quickly came to the attention of the city authorities and the bar owner got a disgruntled call saying they were going to fine him for every single flyer posted. Slipknot apologised profusely to the club promoter for the inconvenience caused, but since they were playing to almost full houses every week, he secretly told them to keep 'flying the town'.

Chapter 2.

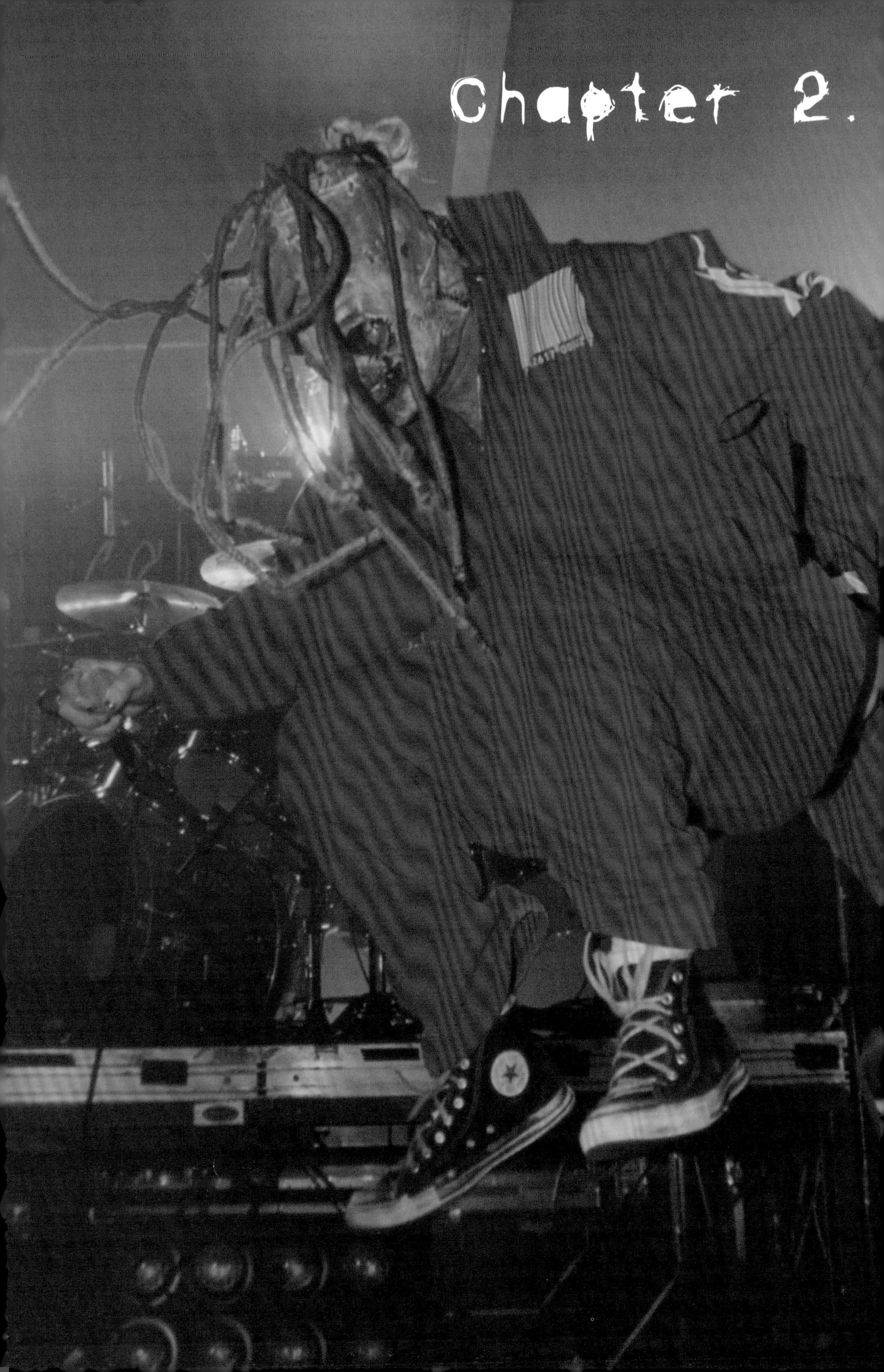

Korn On The Kob

By the end of 1995, Slipknot were starting to create a real buzz in town, so they decided it was about time they entered the studio to get some of their new work down on tape. Although they loved playing live, the band were keen to get a record deal and wanted to have a demo to give to prospective labels. On the off-chance, they invited a producer, Sean McMahon, to a December rehearsal and he was totally blown away by what they were doing. In fact, their talent and musical tightness impressed him so much that he brought them to the attention of Mike Lawyer, owner of local Des Moines recording studio SR Audio.

Sean McMahon saw Slipknot as his pet project and devoted many hours helping to develop their style. They would regularly come into the studio and record a whole different set of ideas that they would then listen to at home and use in rehearsals to perfect what they were doing. By all accounts, it was a turbulent time recording in the cold Des Moines winter. With the tension of putting the sound together and capturing it on tape, tempers were frayed. In fact, Anders and Joey once had a big bust-up with Joey blasting out of the session screaming that he was quitting. Listening to their music day-in-day-out also started to drive Sean McMahon slightly mad and he had to take time out lying on the floor of the control room with his eyes fixed on the ceiling to recover. Despite this, Slipknot were given valuable time to experiment with their sound and provided with the space just to try things out.

In early 1996, the band started to collect all their recorded work together with a view to putting out an album. The tracks were finally mixed in March by Slipknot and McMahon and were later mastered at SR Audio by Sean and owner Mike Lawyer. After much deliberation, the band decided to call their future album *Mate. Feed. Kill. Repeat.* This was meant to represent the complete life-cycle through reproduction and feeding in order to survive, to the killing of enemies before the whole process starts again. As a result of its genesis, the eight-songs (plus a hidden track) that were released ventured down paths that had  never been explored by metal bands before. Although the album lacked a coherent structure, ranging from death-metal and grindcore to funk and disco, it presented a fascinating snapshot of a band in development. Anders' vocals were almost death-metal in delivery, owing much to the style of Sepultura and Soulfly vocalist Max Cavalera. Despite the hotchpotch of different styles, the Slipknot umbrella held the whole thing together. Crucially, with *Mate. Feed. Kill. Repeat.*, the band had also staked their claim to break free from all constraints, to try anything they wanted as long as they could make it their own.

The cover art for the album also marked the group out as something dementedly different. The front picture shows drummer Joey enshrined in a huge metal death cage that was welded together by Shawn and called 'Patiently Awaiting the Jigsaw Flesh'. The insert picture, which had been taken in September 1995, features the band's tattooists Dav-O and Greg (or Cuddles as he was affectionately known). This photo was shot in an alley near the Axiom tattoo parlour and shows a naked Greg with his face inside a steel frame, something that seriously freaked out passers-by at the time.

They had 1000 copies of the album manufactured and it was finally released on Halloween night 1996. In total, the band invested around $40,000 into making, manufacturing and promoting the album, much of which was borrowed by Shawn. This virtually bankrupted the members and they never got close to recouping the money they spent. Ironically, the original copies of the record now exchange hands for as much as $250.

Chapter 3

Game Plan

In the midst of recording and mixing *Mate. Feed. Kill. Repeat.* and before its release, the line-up of the band underwent some major changes. First off, having played guitar on all of the tracks, Donnie found God and decided there was a serious conflict between the group and his new spirituality. He left and was quickly replaced by Craig Jones who had been in Joey's band Modifidious. Craig had been on the fringes of the band throughout the recording sessions and, in addition to engineering, he had also stumped up some of the money to make the album. Soon after, the band decided that Craig's time would be better spent concentrating on samples and keyboard work, so they asked another old friend from Body Pit, Mick Thompson, to join as guitarist.

In the six months prior to the release of *Mate. Feed. Kill. Repeat.* the band played as many live gigs as possible, working hard on incorporating the new members into their sound. Stage shows at this time were renowned for their all-out wackiness, something that Des Moines had never seen before. Gigs would feature such spectacles as Shawn wearing a Barney suit, Mick dressed as Little-Bo-Peep and assorted members attired in ballroom dresses and nuns' habits. This innocent humour was twisted with mad lighting and heavy strobe effects and, of course, dark heavy metal.

During this time, the band also started to wear masks. Shawn owned a clown mask that he had bought years before on the clearance counter of a thrift store and he took to placing it between the front of his toms at every show. During a rehearsal, he decided to put it on and before long the other members started picking out their own masks and bringing them to shows. No one in the band really considered that it would become a permanent fixture within Slipknot, but they soon stuck and became an integral part of the band's appearance. The masks also gave the group a measure of anonymity which they built on by assigning each member a different number. The allocation of these numbers came easily to the band, almost as if they had somehow been chosen for them already. Strange as it may seem, there was absolutely no arguments over which numeral each individual would adopt. While on Slipknot business, the members came to refer to each other by these numbered aliases rather than their names.

In the late fall of 1996, with the record out doing the rounds and news of the band spreading like wildfire across the mid-west, Slipknot took the next big step of their career by entering the local Battle of the Bands competition. This was organised by Sophia John, music director at the central Iowan radio station KKDM 107.5. Like Slipknot, she was also concerned about the lack of a viable music scene in the Des Moines area and wanted to draw the best musicians together, giving them the opportunity of some much needed national exposure. Slipknot submitted some of their demo recordings along with 100 other hopefuls which a committee then whittled down to eight bands. These groups were paired up to play a full set at the Safari Club in front of a judging panel, made up of the great and good of the now developing Des Moines music scene. Slipknot were ecstatic to find themselves one of the chosen few, and in November came up against the more mainstream metal band Stone Sour. On the night in question they pulled out all the stops and put in a blistering performance that just pipped Stone Sour at the post. Taking first place in the competition earned them over $1000 as well as more recording time at SR Audio and a guest spot on KKDM's *Mac and Amy Show*. Crucially, they also impressed Sophia John to such an extent that she made the decision, with the band's full consent, to become their full-time manager, offering her services free of charge.

Under her direction, the band realised that they needed to become a lot more professional about what they were doing. They were keen to

get signed by a major label, but lacked the necessary focus and structure that would enable them to make it big. One part of this new thrust was to undertake some more recording and in the summer of 1997 they went back to SR Audio again with producer Sean McMahon. The band were keen to get the input of the newer members, who had joined after the recording of *Mate. Feed. Kill. Repeat.*, onto tape, especially as they were now such a crucial part of their live shows. They therefore set about recording a mixture of old and newer material, incorporating Craig's sampling and Mick's guitar playing.

As part of trying to effect the transition to become a major label band, they decided that they needed a more radio-friendly voice than that of Anders, who sang in a deep grunting style. Shawn called in Corey Taylor from Stone Sour, the group Slipknot had come up against the year before in the Battle of the Bands. Although Stone Sour's progression was going well, Corey had often considered what it would be like to be a member of Slipknot, and was totally floored when he was asked to join. He felt that he could achieve much more with Slipknot than he ever had with his present band and so jumped ship to join up. This created a problem, though, as Anders was now pushed into the less-

24

er role of backing singer and percussionist. He soon got bored of playing second-fiddle and quit the band publicly on stage at the end of a gig. Although he was bitter about the situation at the time, after a period of licking his wounds he emerged as vocalist for another local band Painface.

With Corey on board, things began to change radically for the group. He brought many new ideas into the camp and contributed greatly to their new direction. The previous experimental styles of jazz, funk and disco were downplayed with a greater reliance on a musically tighter and a more homogeneous rock sound. The band also polished up their stage

show, replacing the wide assortment of costumes with more generic coveralls. This not only made them look more unified but also removed the comic element that had been a feature of the group's earlier performances. These coveralls had the number of each member on the sleeve and sported the barcode 742617000027 which had been assigned to the band for the release of *Mate. Feed. Kill. Repeat.* Determined to set the proverbial cat amongst the pigeons and cause a major stir, they also made their shows sicker and sicker. As time went on, the band kept pushing the boundaries of what their audience would accept. They were determined to stand head and shoulders above the competition and by playing horrifically exciting off-the-cuff gigs they did just that.

With their stage show rocking, the band now had to fill Anders' previous percussion duties. They got in touch with old friend and band tattooist Greg Welts who was well known for being a local headcase. Greg, aka Cuddles, had previously drummed for Joey and Paul in another local band The Have Nots and, as mentioned, he'd appeared on the artwork for *Mate. Feed. Kill. Repeat.* Cuddles hit the band running, smashing up drum sets like there was no tomorrow and hurling them into the crowd. The band further upped the stakes by asking local DJ Sid Wilson to come on board and take care of the turntables.

Up until the summer of 1997, the band had been distributing *Mate. Feed. Kill. Repeat.* themselves, selling copies at gigs and mailing them out to promoters and record labels. They were now on a hunt for a proper distributor and in May they attracted the attention of Dan Schlissel from Ismist Recordings. He had made the three hour trek from Lincoln, Nebraska, to Des Moines to see a number of bands at the Safari Club, a venue which Slipknotter Shawn had bought himself a short time before. When Dan got to the club, one of the acts he had come to see had finished their set and already left the venue. So as not to let a good night go to waste, and being in such a cool venue with a growing reputation he decided to stay for a drink. Over the course of the evening he got chatting with Shawn who told him about Slipknot and gave him a copy of *Mate. Feed. Kill. Repeat.* Dan listened to it all the way home and next day got straight on the phone to Shawn, inviting him and the band's manager Sophia to Lincoln. As a result of that meeting, on the 13th of June 1997 he took over distribution of the remaining 386 copies of the album. He quickly used his contacts to get copies of the CD into chain stores which were tracked by Soundscan, the computerised sales index that major labels and radio stations monitor and that Billboard uses to assemble the US charts. He also put the band on a firmer business footing, taking over what had previously been done by the members, their girl-friends and subsequently Sophia John. As time went on, the group realised that A&R men were constantly attending their gigs and noting their progress with great interest.

With the band going from strength to strength it was rumoured around town that they were going to open a show for Marilyn Manson. The opportunity to support a major act had been one of the perks of winning the Battle of the Bands competition, but the promised gig never materialised. Instead, the band got a chance to play at DotFest '97, which proved to be a real turning point in their career. Their performance, on the 7th of June, not only exposed them to a huge crowd of 12,000 people, far and away their largest audience to date, but also were attending the event. The show was a huge success. Slipknot burst onto the stage throwing tampons into the crowd before going straight into their set which sent the crowd wild. Being such an important gig, they had decided to bring on some additional members, called the 'Gimps', who consisted of various insane friends covered in liquid latex. They had intended to set 'Gimp' Slick Rick on fire, but couldn't get the necessary permits. In spite of this, the mayhem that ensued led to the band being cut off before the end of their set, triggering a riot in the audience. Although this was the first and last time the 'Gimps' appeared with Slipknot, by the end of the show the band had gotten themselves a whole new group of fans. In addition, the response to their performance had not gone unnoticed by the various A&R personnel present.

Chapter 4

Spit It Out

With their album gaining wider distribution and explosive live shows earning them a solid reputation in rock circles, it was not long before Slipknot caught the attention of several major record companies and producers. When label reps came to Des Moines to check out the group at their best, live on stage, they were always treated to an unorthodox form of post-gig hospitality. The band members knew that the city had little in the way of after-show entertainment, other than the local strip clubs. These establishments therefore became 'de rigeur' in the attempt to persuade these movers and shakers (albeit limited to the male variety) to sign the band up. After hosting guest upon guest, the band were completely burnt out and to this day no one in Slipknot can face stepping inside a strip club again.

But the group started to get some serious offers and were having a hard time deciding who to sign with. On one occasion they were about to go with Epic, when a senior staffer saw them perform and was totally shocked, dropping them immediately. It was then that the band came to the attention of nu-metal guru Ross Robinson.

If the name Ross Robinson means little to you, then you haven't been paying much attention to the heaviest music of the late 1990s. Starting with his ground-breaking production on Korn's first two albums, Robinson has gone on to work with some of the best names in modern rock'n'roll and has recorded a host of albums that have defined the sound of the decade's heavy metal, including those by Limp Bizkit and Soulfly.

The Slipknot members had all been big fans of Robinson's work but had never dreamt that they might actually end up working with him. But when the Masked Marauders were invited to perform on a radio show with another band, Goldfinger, they found out that Robinson was in fact the group's manager. The Slipknotters used this connection to their advantage and got a tape to him. Ross loved their music and visited Des Moines to meet them at a rehearsal. In fact, the guys were so freaked that Robinson was coming to see them that, in spite of the freezing weather, they were all looking out for him on the porch. When his car drew up their courage suddenly faded and they legged it inside. After spending the evening with them, he came back a month or two later to see them at a sell-out show in Des Moines. He was further impressed by what he now saw and offered to finance a new album himself and put it out on his fledgling Roadrunner imprint I Am Records. However, once Roadrunner themselves knew that Robinson was involved, they sent down their A&R chief Monte Conner to check things out. Monte informed his colleagues back at the label that they just had to sign Slipknot. Although there were bigger deals on the table at the time, Slipknot agreed to sign with Roadrunner because of their single minded dedication to all things metal. Some of Slipknot's future label-mates at Roadrunner would include such modern metallic luminaries as Fear Factory, Coal Chamber, Soulfly, and Spineshank. Apart from being home to bands they loved, Roadrunner also offered them a seven album deal worth $500,000.

Having busted their collective asses for two years, playing throughout the mid-west, developing their music, their lyrics, and their overall concept, Slipknot had shown the local rock fans that they were more than just another small time rock band. They now had to prove themselves worthy of the big time and got down to recording their first major label album. As part of this process, the band decided that Cuddles was not really up to it. He had been notoriously unreliable and they felt he was just not dedicated enough to come with them on the next stage of their journey. In addition, he hadn't really added anything new to the sound and instead had just replicated the percussion parts that Anders had previously played. Around the same time he was also fired from his job at the Axiom tattoo shop and went on to leave Des Moines for good, moving to South Dakota to open his own shop there called The Ultimate Prick. He was subsequently replaced by current percussionist Chris Fehn.

In October 1998, with Robinson at their side, the band entered the Cole Rehearsal Studio in Los Angeles for a weeks pre-production. From here they went straight into the Indigo Ranch recording studio in Malibu to preserve forever their new sound. Going straight for the jugular and pulling out all the stops, Robinson managed instantly to capture the band's rampant creative hunger. Their enthusiasm was so great that by the end of the first day's recording they had laid down seven songs. Indeed, if Robinson hadn't forced them to stop playing, they might have recorded the whole album in one night. After years of pent-up rage and utter frustration, Slipknot were clearly ready to get it all out and used these sessions as a cleansing process. In an attempt to assist the band in this, Robinson became just as crazy as the Slipknot wrecking crew — slamming so hard that his pants would fall off. He punched band members in the face, shouted at them and even threw a potted plant at the drummer. Such was both the physical and mental demands of proceedings in the studio, that Robinson got up early every day to work out in the gym, just so he could be in the best shape possible to do the record.

Ross Robinson also had a big impact on the Slipknot sound and created a substantially different album from the more eclectic and experimental *Mate. Feed. Kill. Repeat.* The members had previously refused to accept any musical input from people outside the band, but in the hands of the master they were happy to let him mould the sound as he saw fit. Ross preserved all the basic riffs but to keep the record moving forward he cut out parts of songs that didn't help achieve this. He

also removed all of the funky guitar work, stripped down much of the drumming to make it more powerful and reduced the more detailed technical percussion. Despite these changes, Ross always let the band have the final say. If, for example, there was a cut they didn't like or a guitar effect that they hated, he would change them without arguing. In addition to making a very clean, very raw, heavy no-messing album, Ross helped the band return to the purity of vision that they had started out with. He drew out of them exactly the kind of music they had always wanted to produce. So much so that he achieved the accolade of tenth member.

Chapter 5

Rampaging Remedy

After six weeks of recording, the album was finally wrapped up in early 1999. But just before it was finished, Josh unexpectedly left the group. Although it has been reported that he left because he wanted to spend more time with his family instead of promoting the record, Josh himself says that this is simply not true. The real reason that he left remains a private matter between him and the rest of the band. He certainly did not quit under bad circumstances as he remains good friends with Slipknot and still hangs out with them whenever they return to town. Despite this, it did leave the group with a problem. Although Josh had played on 18 tracks of the new album, there was still more work to be done. As a result, Corey got in touch with another close friend, Jim Root, who had played in the local groups Deadfront and Atomic Opera, and asked him to join Slipknot. He was more than keen to replace Josh and the band returned to the studio with him in February to record one final track for the album, 'Purity'.

Slipknot's hugely anticipated, self-titled, official label debut was finally released on the 29th of June 1999. With barely a mention in the mainstream music press, and only minor airplay on local radio stations, the cult of Slipknot had still spread like a raging disease across the States. The album became the fastest selling debut in Roadrunner Records' history, shifting more than 100,000 copies in the first ten weeks of its release and going Platinum within three months. *Slipknot* the album was proving the perfect antidote for legions of grudge-bearing youths who were turning to the group for solace without even knowing what the band looked like behind their masks and anonymous work-suits.

From the earthy mayhemic metal of '(Sic)' and the relentless sense-bludgeoning overload of 'Surfacing', with its furious scratching, flaying double bass drum and Corey Taylor's Jonathan Davis-style invective vocal, to the heavenly and meaty melodies of 'Wait And Bleed', the album is a creative triumph. The mesmerising rhythmic motion of 'Prosthetics' is particularly eccentric, building from an eerie opening into a claustrophobic, dense wall of sound with Taylor screeching like a tearful felon on his way to a death-row date with the electric chair. Elsewhere in its gruesome grooves, the twisted and roaring rampage of 'Eyeless' provided one of the album's most defining musical moments with Corey bellowing that you can't see California without Marlon Brando's eyes. All this over thunderous rhythmic barrages and painful scalp-cutting guitars. But nothing tops the closing track 'Scissors', which is one of the most genuinely terrifying pieces of music ever recorded. As Taylor chants, everyone sets about detuning their instruments at once, until the track ultimately collapses into complete chaos. When he begins breathing unhinged threats in your face, it becomes the aural equivalent of having a broken pint glass held against your throat by the local headcase.

Although Ross Robinson produced a version of the nu-metal anthem 'Spit It Out', it did not make it onto the final album. Despite re-recording the track three times at Indigo Ranch, Roadrunner decided that they

preferred an earlier version of the song that had been produced by Sean McMahon at SR Audio. As the result of a printing error, the album unfortunately mis-credited Robinson as producer rather than McMahon, even though Ross actually had nothing to do with this recording. This error was later corrected on the subsequent CD single release. In addition, it is a little known fact that several of the bonus tracks on the UK and Japanese releases of the album were also recorded at SR Audio by McMahon and not by Robinson. A few copies of the album also exist which feature the songs 'Frail Limb Nursery' and the Korn-like 'Purity', both of which are about a girl named Purity Knight, who had been buried alive. Slipknot found details about this incident on an internet crimesite but, after Roadrunner released the CD, it turned out that the incident was actually a copyrighted story. To prevent them from being sued by the author, both tracks were removed from the album and Slipknot were forced to re-release the record with a replacement cut entitled 'Me Inside'.

The thoroughly unpleasant and truly unforgettable *Slipknot* was the quintessential nu-metal sound of 1999. Capturing their catalytic, live sound perfectly, the band's major label debut was almost as enthralling as their extravagant stage performances. The tracks flowed together in a strangely smooth, yet aggressive manner lying somewhere between *Mega-Mix* and *Sgt. Pepper*, creating a kind of destructive audio-verity that is hugely spellbinding. Not only does each track have its own feel, but the choice of background sound effects are also highly original. In every second of every song you can almost hear the hatred and frustration that springs from Slipknot's upbringing. Venomous, apoplectic and vein-poppingly furious, the pure intense sound and nihilistic, atmospheric lyrical vibe is clearly the result of a sterile environment that normally fails to nurture or inspire any creativity in the masses.

Chapter 6.

Sonic Sickos

Just before the album was released, Slipknot took the rock world by storm at Ozzfest 1999. As far as 'commercial' national exposure was concerned, this broke them wide open across the United States. Ask any member of the band and they'll tell you that Ozzfest was probably the best thing that could have happened to Slipknot. Despite the fact that they hadn't even released their major label debut, they had the undying support of rock business queen Sharon Osbourne, Ozzy's wife, who specifically picked them to tour as part of this prestigious metal package. She took the gamble and gave them the support they needed to jump out at mainstream America on that summer's touring trek. They appeared alongside some of metal's biggest names - Rob Zombie, Godsmack, Slayer, The Deftones, Primus, System Of A Down, Fear Factory, Drain, STH, and its headliners, the legendary Black Sabbath. The response to the band on these festival dates was overwhelming as the nine-piece group pummelled crowds all over the US and made many new friends and enemies along the way. Slipknot were indeed the Ozzfest's dark-horse victors as they stole the show with their unique audio-visual nightmare.

With the Ozzfest behind them, the men of Slipknot were soon setting their sights on other musical endeavours. After wrapping up the tour, Slipknot singer Corey Taylor made a beeline for a Malibu recording studio where he joined Sticky Fingaz of Onyx to record a song called 'End Of The World'. The pair joined Slipknot producer Ross Robinson in his Indigo Ranch recording studio to lay down the track, which was scheduled to appear on the upcoming solo effort from Sticky. On the 19th of August Slipknot then made an unforgettable guest appearance on the *Howard Stern Show*. Even the unshockable king of the shock-jocks was left bewildered by their antics which included DJ Sid Wilson masturbating in the corner of the studio while another member of the band crapped in a bucket as a memento of their visit.

In the fall of 1999 the Kamikaze Nine got straight back into touring smaller sized venues with fellow Roadrunner acts Coal Chamber and Machine Head, in what was billed as the Livin' La Vida Loca Tour. With the arrival of the year 2000, Slipknot embarked on the next leg of their US tour. They lined up a string of Stateside dates with Canadian teenage female grindcore quartet Kittie and kicked off on New Year's day in their hometown. The first part of the tour didn't pass without incident as on the 11th of January, the masked metallers refused to go on stage in Oklahoma City. The band's fans took the news kind of hard and stirred up a minor flurry of destruction. When the tour (which by this point also included Will Haven on the bill) arrived at Oklahoma City's Tower Theatre, it was discovered that the crowd of ticket-holders exceeded the maximum number allowed under the building's fire regulations. As a result, the local fire marshal refused to let the gig go ahead unless twenty people were removed from the audience. Of course, when Slipknot learned that fans were being forced to leave the venue and the whole ticket-holding 'family' was not going to be there, they refused to go on. The police beefed up their presence with dogs and helicopters as the now unhappy crowd tore up parts of the club before spilling into the street. Fixtures, chairs, and even structures rooted in cement were among the items damaged.

Other than this fiasco, things have been looking pretty damn good for Slipknot. With little support from mainstream rock radio or MTV, the band still managed to promote their debut album and achieve huge sales. Their steady diet of touring began to pay off when the Recording Industry Association of America (RIAA) gave a gold certification to their 1999 self-titled debut for selling more than 500,000 copies. They also got some more good news when their home video *Welcome To Our Neighbourhood* bettered efforts by Madonna and Shania Twain, landing Slipknot at the top of the Billboard music video charts. This Slipknot celluloid offering carries live performance footage, interviews, and the seldom-seen video for 'Spit It Out', the first release from the band's *Slipknot* album, which was banned from MTV. In celebration, the band staged a mainstream coming-out party of sorts on the 25th of February, with their network television debut on NBC's *Late Night With Conan O'Brien*. They were by far the heaviest band to have played on the show and in addition to breaking down a lot of barriers, they gained themselves a whole new legion of fans.

Slipknot then kept the touring momentum going by heading over to Europe for shows in several major cities. In London, they also put in a much-talked about 'meet-and-greet' appearance at the Virgin Megastore. This came after competitive retailer HMV had forced them to cancel a string of British in-store appearances due to concerns over the number and nature of Slipknot fans. By the end of March, though, Slipknot had prematurely pulled the plug on their European trek. Having been on the road almost constantly since Summer 1999, the constant touring, in-store appearances and press interviews had really taken their toll and the band were simply exhausted. With twelve dates remaining on their itinerary, they took time out and headed back to the US.

Chapter 7.

Tattoo The Earth

In late October 1999, Slipknot looked poised to keep all this momentum going by delivering their second video for the track 'Wait and Bleed' to MTV. The audio for this release was a more radio-friendly version than that on the album and was remixed by Terry Date. The accompanying video, which drew its inspiration from the 1989 cult horror movie *Puppet Master*, consisted of miniature stop-motion animated Slipknot figures running amok in a toy store. After airing ten times on MTV, the band recalled the video, stating that it was not a proper representation of Slipknot. They soon replaced it with a more straight-up performance clip that captured the band during a homecoming gig in Iowa, recorded during the summer of 1999. Despite this rapid reversal, the remixed version of the track was released as a single in Europe and in January 2000 was included on the movie soundtrack for *Scream 3*.

A brief Canadian outing at this time also proved eventful when percussionist Shawn Crahan got into a fight with a spectator at the band's Montreal show. The fan, who had been making rude gestures and egging him on to come down and fight, got a fistful of trouble when the Slipknot skinsman hit him square in the face. The group also held a costume contest for their fans at a Toronto record store for which the dedicated many were asked to dress up like their favourite band member (mask, jump-suit and all). The members of the group then judged who was the best, handing out a range of prizes including tickets to the band's show, trading cards, a Slipknot skateboard and an autographed poster.

In early March 2000, while being interviewed on MTV's *The Return of the Rock*, Slipknot rubbished any notions that they would be performing again at that year's upcoming Ozzfest festival. What they did have up their sleeves was something far more spectacular. Following the success of their Ozzfest 1999 performance, Slipknot would team up with a host of other like-minded acts for the first annual Tattoo The Earth touring trek, which was set to kick off that summer. The idea of this tour had come from the minds of New York's Beat Co. (who would also be responsible for producing the event) and The Agency Group (who would also be booking the tour). The Agency Group already counted Slipknot among its hard rock clients.

It was also rumoured that Slipknot would be playing alongside Limp Bizkit on the 2000 Family Values tour. This only proved to be hearsay as Slipknot were exclusively committed to the Tattoo The Earth live extravaganza. The band also pulled out of playing on MTV's early summer Return Of The Rock tour. Although there were rumours of disagreements between Slipknot and Crazy Town, who had also been scheduled to appear, as it turned out, the band simply didn't want to commit to MTV. They did manage to re-schedule their infamous cancelled show in Oklahoma

City and line themselves up for a European trip prior to their Dynamo Festival appearance at Nijmegen, Holland in June 2000, playing alongside Korn, Suicidal Tendencies, Kittie, P.O.D. and Sevendust. Slipknot also donated the song 'Spit It Out' for inclusion on a CD companion to MTV's daily metal showcase *The Return Of The Rock*. This was set for release on Roadrunner Records later that year and featured the Slipknot track among metallic brain-teasers from a host of other hard rock heavyweights, including Kid Rock, Korn, Coal Chamber and Machine Head.

Springtime 2000 saw the masked chameleons change colour. Slipknot confirmed that they were now to deck themselves out in white, bright blue, and brown jump-suits which would carry several new visual features. These included a '6(sic)6' on the arm, a Tribal 'S' and barcodes, as well as numbers and letters which were embroidered on for a better look. At around the same time, filming began for an upcoming home video with a working title of *Assess The (Sic)ness*. This was set to feature at least three full-length shows, including one gig in Del Mar which was almost caught on camera but was cancelled after a few numbers due to electrical problems. Needless to say, the band got a little angry at this and vented their collective spleen by lighting fires.

After a short period in which some Slipknot members succumbed to illness, the band continued their tour including radio-station-sponsored shows such as the WHFStival gig in Washington, D.C. on Memorial Day weekend. The group also headlined the main stage at the X-Fest in Float Rite Park, Somerset, Wisconsin which saw them on the same weekend bill as stoner rock gurus Stone Temple Pilots and pop rock indie punksters Everclear.

On the 15th July 2000, Slipknot played their first gig in Portland Oregon as part of the inaugural 30-date summer Tattoo The Earth tour of major US cities. This rampage was set to include 14 of rock's heaviest hitters including Slayer, Sevendust, Sepultura, Nashville Pussy, (hed) pe, Downset and Spineshank. They would be spread across two stages, with a host of henna artists, body piercers, and tattooists actually on stage in between sets. Among the men providing the ink were Sean Vasquez (who had tattooed Howard Stern as well as members of the Sex Pistols and Kiss) and Paul Booth (who had worked on members of Limp Bizkit, Pantera, and the Deftones as well as The Undertaker of the World Wrestling Federation). Tattoo The Earth's maiden voyage at the Portland Meadows Amphitheatre saw some 16,000 fans descend on the arena to sample the tour's celebration of heavy music and body art. This initial Oregon show also found Tattoo The Earth teaming up with KUFO-FM's annual Rockfest which also brought the Stone Temple Pilots to the bill as the closing band in the days entertainment.

The whole show was a riot of confusion after Coal Chamber cancelled at the last minute, throwing the carefully ordered schedule into disarray, with the crowd's shouting drowning out the host DJ. After Slayer had finished playing, a curious hush descended on the drunken hoards who now waited in virtual silence for Slipknot. As the food kiosks closed and fans started to swell around the main stage, a solo vocal track was played through the speakers, building up to sampled religious lyrics that descended into the repetition of the word Satan over and over again. Slipknot then burst onto the stage and the crowd went wild with mad extreme moshing, kicking out and punching those around them. The band climbed the speakers, diving sixty foot into the crowd, smashing drums and hurling the debris around the stage. If the calibre of

their initial tour compatriots was not enough of a mark as to how far Slipknot had come, on the 20th of July, the monsters of rock, Metallica, topped the Tattoo The Earth bill 'for one night only' at the Giants Stadium in East Rutherford, New Jersey.

The tour's stop at the Float-Rite Park in Somerset, Wisconsin on the 28th of July was an eventful one, thanks to a backstage melee involving members of Slipknot, One Minute Silence, Hatebreed, and the security hired for the event. The altercation, which took place next to the band's tour bus, began when Slipknot percussionist Shawn Crahan, his drum technician, and One Minute Silence frontman Brian 'Yap' Barry were allegedly accosted by security while riding around in a motorised golf cart. Metal band Hatebreed, who had been preparing to go on stage for their set, then jumped in to help out members of the other bands. When pressed for a comment, Slipknot's label rep claimed no knowledge of the event, while a spokesperson for One Minute Silence played down the incident attributing it to a 'misunderstanding'. According to security, the posse had been endangering people in the area with the golf cart and had repeatedly refused to stop the vehicle, responding to requests to do so with obscene gestures. Slipknot considered cancelling their appearance, though the band did go on to perform that evening and complied with a request not to discuss the event from the stage in case it further riled the audience. The band and their Tattoo The Earth counterparts eventually wrapped up the tour in Phoenix, Arizona, in late August, with Slipknot heading off to Europe for some festival shows. As an enduring souvenir of the trek, a live album entitled *Tattoo The Earth: The First Crusade*, would hit record stores in the fall of 2000, providing a needy fix of live Slipknot in the shape of 'Liberate'.

Chapter 8.

Attitude and Craft

At root, the underlying aesthetic behind Slipknot can be summed up in one word: respect. They respect other people for who they are and what they do, as long as they stay true to themselves. Slipknot don't talk and sing about religion or politics; as far as they're concerned, it is up to individuals to decide their own views on these issues. Additionally, they will not be swayed by others. They know their own minds and stick to their own principles.

This fiercely independent streak manifests itself in their lyrics which predominantly deal with personal pain, inner experience and various events that have touched their lives. For example, the song 'Eyeless' came about after a visit to New York when Slipknot were about to close the Roadrunner deal. During the trip Shawn and Corey passed a homeless man on the street who was screaming over and over that it was impossible to see California without Marlon Brando's eyes. This perversity appealed to them and ended up as the basis for the subsequent song lyric. Likewise, while web-surfing, Corey came across the story of Purity Knight, a 20-year-old girl who was buried alive by an ex-lover. This affected Corey so much that he had a nightmare about it, something he later expressed in the contentious song 'Purity'. In fact, dreams are a constant source of inspiration and the song 'Wait and Bleed' came from a dream Corey had about being in a bathtub filled with blood from his slit wrists. The band refuse to preach to their audience and prefer talking to them on their level, treating them as equals. This can be illustrated best through the anthemic track 'Surfacing' in which they advise their fans not to worry about other people judging them but to stick to what they believe in.

This attitude also carries directly over into their collective music-making. Slipknot have always played the music that they want to and have never set out to cater to any particular audience. Although the band have obvious influences, their pure, individual, artistic expression has enabled them to create something strikingly original. One can draw analogies between Slipknot and Rage Against the Machine, Pantera, Gwar, Kiss or Metallica, but apart from the metallic distorted guitars and their nastiness, the similarities are not really that great. Their music is undoubtedly heavy and with nine members there are certainly a lot of influences present, but Slipknot also inject a host of refreshingly new styles into the mix from jungle and rave to disco and funk.

The band feel that many of the comparisons that are drawn are simply the result of sloppy and lazy writing by journalists, and are not borne out by a close listening to Slipknot's music. The name The Insane Clown Posse often comes up in comparison, but this is clearly due to the use of masks by both groups and musically they have little in common. Of all the bands they could be compared to, Ross Robinson's protégés, the mighty Korn is probably the most accurate. But although they do share a thudding guitar attack, and their songs deal with similarly disturbing subject matter, they never sound that close. Moreover, Corey Taylor's vocal technique, alternating between melodic choruses, whispered/moaned pre-choruses and flat-out, distorted hollering, could be seen as drawing on the style of Korn's Jonathan Davis, but when stacked against the contributions of the eight instrumentalists in Slipknot, the sound becomes totally unique.

Another area where Slipknot are true pioneers is in the line-up of the band. Boasting a steady nine-piece ensemble consisting of not one, but three prominent percussionists, two gritty guitarists, a ballsy bass player, a demented DJ, a mad sampler and a psychopathic singer, the aggressive wall of percussive throb and crunching guitars is enough to defuse and destroy most electrical equipment within range. The drums are at the very heart of the band and Slipknot have been consistently beat-heavy since their earliest conception. The group is organised around a drumming triangle with Shawn playing on the hard left and Chris on the hard right, while Joey, the main drummer, sits at the back thrashing the living daylights out of his acoustic kit. He grounds the band with a rock-steady beat that is augmented by fast double-bass drum lines. The two percussionists then add an assortment of drums, kegs, cans, chopsaws and much more, which gives them a different sound layer to Joey. Sean tends to play more aggressive power patterns while Chris adds the tribal sounds into the mix, both cutting their drumming down to basics, eschewing anything over-fancy or technical for the sake of backing up the straight beats. This surround-sound drumming is boosted by the appearance of Corey in the middle, while the guitar players Mick and James stand on either side of him. Paul comes in on bass a little behind Corey with Craig on keyboards and sampling equipment. Craig uses these to trigger weird sound effects, movie clips and pre-recorded song introductions, while DJ Sid Wilson adds cool beats and scratches from his turntables.

The whirlwind vibe that this line-up creates is truly terrifying. Although 'The Knot' have all the essential nu-metal ingredients in place: down-tuned churning guitar riffs, a subterranean heavy bass that could rearrange your innards, explosively clattering hip-hop inspired drumming and a stream-of-conscious, multi-octave psychobabble, their wicked hooks and melodic sensibilities set them well apart from their like-minded contemporaries. With their creepy, hypnotic, unnerving

loops, the horror-show element of the band is exaggerated, as sirens
whine and tribal drums batter in unexpected and dizzyingly polyrhyth-
mic ways. Not only excellent musicians, they also have a sense of
camaraderie, sometimes playing together as tightly as a big-band jazz
ensemble. They all seem able to express the same focus simultaneously.

With so many members in the band, you may be wondering how they actually manage to get anything done, especially as they always rehearse
and perform with all members present. The reason that Slipknot works is
that each and every member is totally dedicated to the band. Although
they operate on democratic principles and respect each other's opin-
ions, individuals do inevitably take on different responsibilities, for
example when dealing with the press. This division of labour also carries over into the writing of material. Everyone in the band is free
to write words or music but some members, such as Paul and Joey, take
on the bulk of the writing. Despite this, songs are usually worked up
as a band effort in rehearsal to which everyone contributes. First of
all the 'core' group of Mick, Jim, Joey and Paul will work on a new
songs structure, building up the guitar, bass and drums and then they
will add the extra DJ beats and samples as and when they are needed.

Quite often songs will simply develop from
jamming, for instance 'Eyeless' started with a
beat Sid spun from his turntables. Once the
music is completed, it is often Corey who
works on the lyrics. With nine people con-
tributing, this un-egoistic writing formula
works surprisingly well. The band are realis-
tic and do not mind sitting out for a track if
their part does not fit. Of course this just
leaves them free to rampage the stage egging
on the crowd.

Blending intense rhythms and scorching blast
beats with twisted samples and sassy sonic
scratching has become the norm for this band.
They combine every element that has made metal
heavy, and they do it with a precision that is
so far unparalleled in the modern heavy rock
community. With a wide array of influences
ranging from the speed thrash of Slayer to the
plastic panache pop of The Police, and back to
the gruesome grind-gore of Cannibal Corpse, Slipknot are a cosmic
blender. Although it's not hard to find elements of their music that
one can appreciate for its genuine craft and musicianship, many fans
are attracted to them for the pure intensity of sound that distinguishes
them from all other musical acts. No other current group comes close to
matching Slipknot's sonic brand of complex, violent heavy-metal, hard-
core and hip-hop.

Chapter 9.

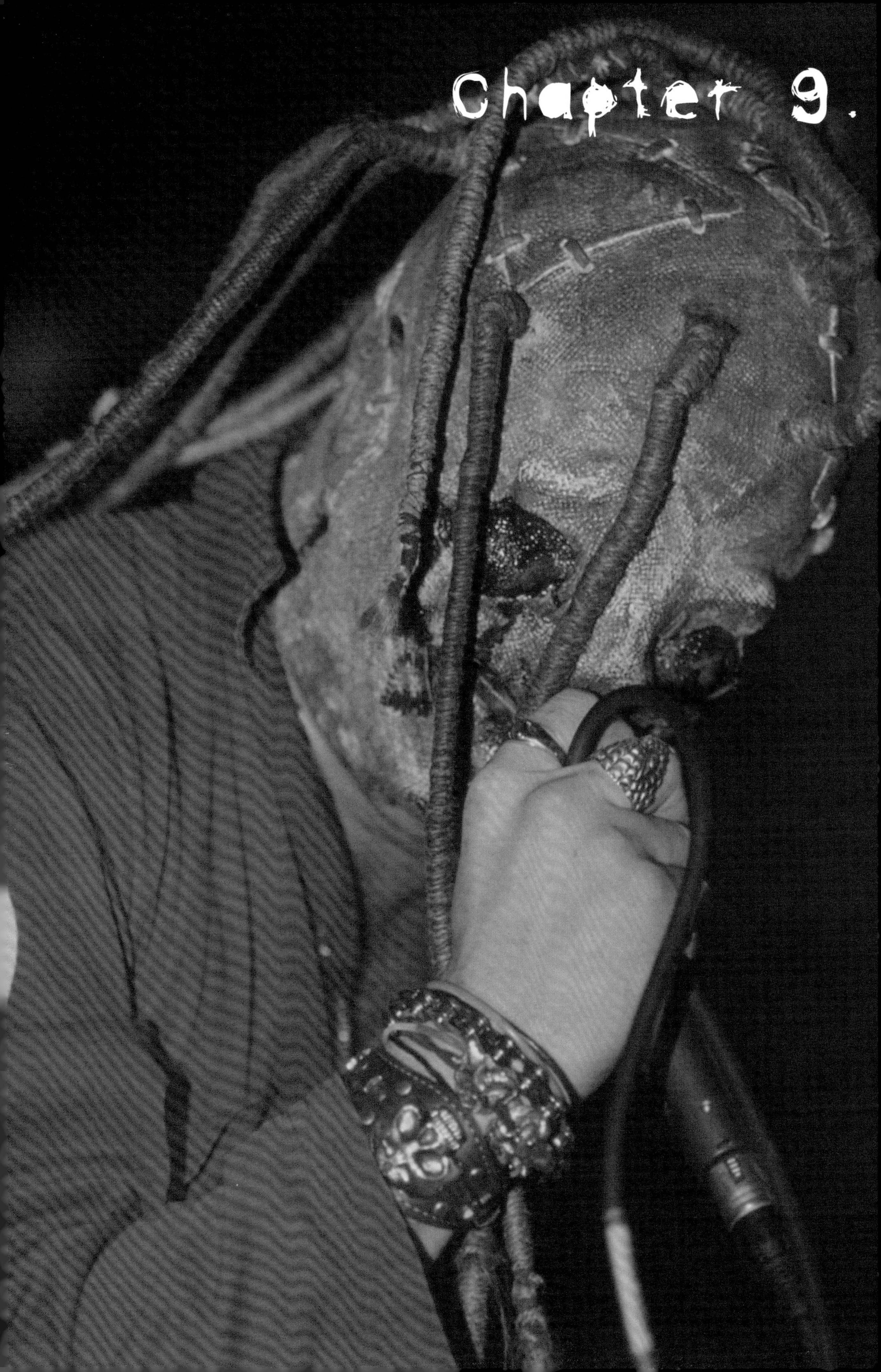

Audio/Visual Nightmare

Live performance is at the heart of what Slipknot is about. Part of the motivation for starting the band, and an aim that has stayed true to this day, is the desire to put on a complete show. They sensed in the early days that people didn't just want to look at a group of musicians playing, and so they set about creating a complete audio and visual experience. Although recording is one thing, the true Slipknot experience is to see them live. They perform aggressively onstage, yet are professional and accurate, even though their gripping live shows are a free-for-all of chaos and cataclysmic craziness. Such is the adrenaline rush they create that they have no need for fancy explosions, laser lights or big backdrops. Their shows are about getting the audience to bleed their anger, release their frustrations and forget their resentment. With the crowd creating their own vibe, the band in turn feed off it, creating a continuous circle that explodes in a symbiotic transference of escalating angst.

While most of their live audience are over 18 years of age, Slipknot believe it is important to reach rock fans of all ages, especially as many under 18's sneak in to see the band's shows. Since their formation in the mid-1990s, Slipknot have slowly developed a kind of one-on-one relationship with their fans. The fact that they speak to younger enthusiasts in a language that most metal bands don't, means that they have attracted many dedicated and fanatical followers from this age group. Presenting equal parts theatre and volume, based on something completely and utterly unique, Slipknot is pure excitement for such teenagers. The kids who see themselves as rebels and outsiders identify themselves with the group, not only for what the band feel, but also for what they have come to represent. Besides standing outside every show for hours, meeting and greeting their fans, thanking as many as possible for attending and letting them know they are all appreciated, the band also walk around the audience after gigs and talk to people. The fact that, unmasked, they can mix with the crowd incognito and gauge the audience reaction by pretending just to be fans themselves, gives Slipknot an edge by creating feedback and a nice line in market research.

With the band feeding off the audience and vice versa, some unforgettable moments are inevitable. In addition to the group running around the stage causing as much mayhem as possible, moshing and roughhousing with other members of the band, jumping off speakers and balconies, Sid and Chris often get into fights which can spill over to the other musicians and sometimes into the crowd. The intense heat that the band generate inside their stage clothes is said to often cause them heat-stroke, which makes them wilder than ever. On one notable occasion, it was a head wound and not heat-stroke that sent a member of Slipknot to hospital. Following their Ozzfest 1999 performance at the PNC Bank Centre in Holmdel, New Jersey, percussionist Shawn Crahan struck his head against

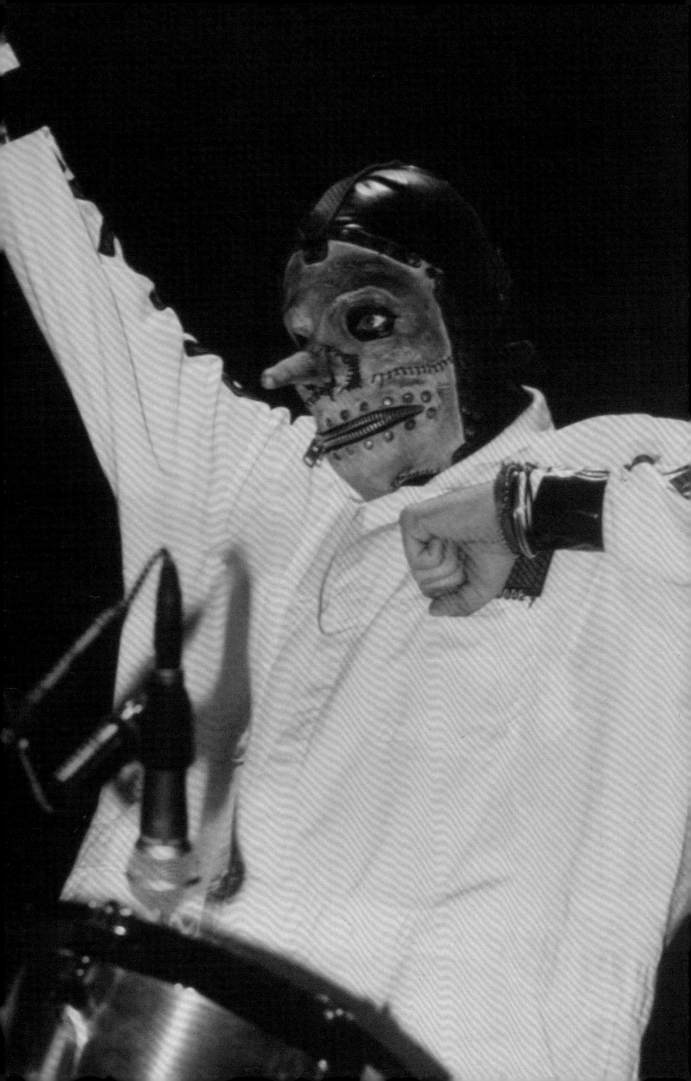

his drum kit. The blow came ironically during the second song of the band's set, 'Eyeless', and left Crahan with a nasty gash over his left eye. Clad in his trademark clown mask and jump-suit, the drummer actually managed to finish the set, despite temperatures that soared into the high 90s. Such was his dedication to all things Slipknot that he even had time to sign a few autographs before he was whisked off to Holmdel's Bayshore Hospital, where he received five stitches to close the wound.

These kinds of injuries are par for the course with Slipknot members. In addition to the above, Shawn has also fractured his knuckles, severed a finger, broken his collarbone, bruised his pelvic bone and slipped discs. On one occasion, Sid even set himself on fire when he inadvertently squirted some lighter fuel on his leg while trying to ignite Chris's drums. This was quickly put out, but not before it singed a large portion of his body hair. With the stage becoming a war zone, the audience are sometimes on the receiving end. One notorious incident occurred at Wolverhampton's Civic Hall, in the English Midlands, during August 2000. Sid back-flipped off a 30-foot high balcony and landed right on top of a fan, 19-year-old Lyndsey Pearce. She suffered head and spinal injuries as well as severe concussion. Sid was understandably distressed and even went to visit her in hospital.

Slipknot love making their show as sick as possible. At one stage they used to carry around a dead crow which Shawn had found in his driveway. This was placed in a large pickle jar where it slowly decomposed, turning into a mushy mess. He used to bring it to shows and would open the jar during the band's set, take an almighty inhale and subsequently throw up all over his mask and jumpsuit. He would then give it to kids who would dip their hands in, wipe it on their faces and puke as well. When a couple of fans broke the jar open and desecrated its sanctity by playing ball with it, the band decided it was about time they got rid of it. On another occasion, Corey and Shawn received a severed beaver tail from a police officer who, strangely enough, thought they would appreciate it as a gift. As soon as they got it on stage they started putting it in their mouths and squeezing the fluids onto their faces and bodies. Needless to say, they also ended up puking their guts out. This kind of spontaneity is right at the core of a live Slipknot show. While they are out there on stage, anything is possible and there is nothing they won't do to release the anger from their systems. The band say that after gigs, when they reflect on what they have done, they can scarcely believe it's happened.

Chapter 10

Behind the Masks

In addition to their massive sound, Slipknot are best known for their spectacular, freaky, demonic-looking masks, customised to each member's particular design. Although this odd assortment of bondage hoods, horror-movie facials and other bizarre types of headgear is unusual, the use of masks is certainly nothing new in the field of entertainment. Shakespeare used masks for his characters way back in the 16th century, and indeed the two-mask symbol has become the accepted image to represent the theatre in general. But what about contemporary music? The best known wearers of masks in recent times have been New York's most notorious band Kiss, who favoured a glam-rock stylisation created largely with makeup. But although they had a very striking image when they first appeared in 1974, and nothing like it had been seen before, when compared to the aggressive and explosive reactions brought on by the sight of Slipknot, their look now seems tame and even elegant.

Many Slipknot fans are understandably keen to see pictures of the band unmasked, but the group claim not to wear the masks simply to keep their identities secret. In fact, the members are not really that anonymous at all. Not only are they well known in Des Moines, but they actually only wear their masks at concerts, photo shoots and press conferences. Although they are reluctant when asked for a picture, at Slipknot gigs one can often see them unmasked, meeting and talking with fans. In fact, the anonymity factor is only the by-product of the real mask-wearing objective, which is to create a situation where audiences focus on their music and not their appearance. The masks are striking, but once seen, they stop being an issue and fans pay attention to the music rather than the face behind it.

Slipknot also maintain that they are not hiding behind the masks, believing instead that they actually reveal more of their inner-selves to the audience than one might think. They claim the masks are extensions of their 'real' personalities and that every member lives out their fantasies through the masks they choose to put on. They go inside themselves, picking the face they wear because deep down it reflects their true character. In addition, the masks actually cause the band physical pain, which in turn allows their inner demons to be released more readily, adding to the intensity and aggressiveness of their music. For these reasons the group have no plans to do a 'Slipknot Unmasked Tour', a la Kiss's reunion in the mid-80's. They reckon that the day the masks come off is the day the band folds.

Actually, the gruesome mask-wearing is just a part of the band's wider 'anti-image' message. Through the wearing of generic bar-coded boiler suits and head coverings, the group mute the traditional rock-star image and rebel against the rampant commercialism of modern music. They

consider that this also removes a lot of their ego, enabling them to
remain grounded so they can concentrate on their music. They refuse to
take on the common practice of picking up large endorsements, going
out with movie stars and featuring in television commercials. As Shawn
says, once you have come to terms with him being the Clown, then you
don't worry about how much he weighs, what piercings
he has or what band shirt he is wearing. Indeed,
it is hard to name-drop a barcode.

Of course it would be naive to expect a modern rock
band like Slipknot to isolate themselves totally from
commercial concerns. Out of financial necessity, the band
do have sponsorship for their guitars and produce band merchandise,
but this is all on a limited scale and is strictly controlled by the
group themselves. Indeed, Shawn and Joey design many of the band's

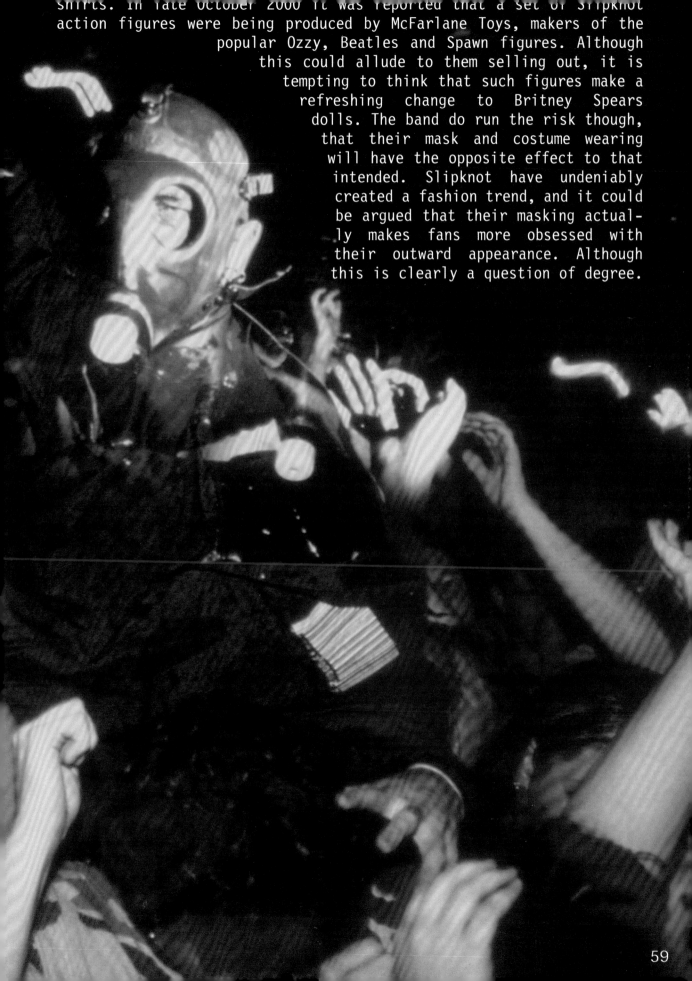

shirts. In late October 2000 it was reported that a set of Slipknot action figures were being produced by McFarlane Toys, makers of the popular Ozzy, Beatles and Spawn figures. Although this could allude to them selling out, it is tempting to think that such figures make a refreshing change to Britney Spears dolls. The band do run the risk though, that their mask and costume wearing will have the opposite effect to that intended. Slipknot have undeniably created a fashion trend, and it could be argued that their masking actually makes fans more obsessed with their outward appearance. Although this is clearly a question of degree.

Chapter 11.

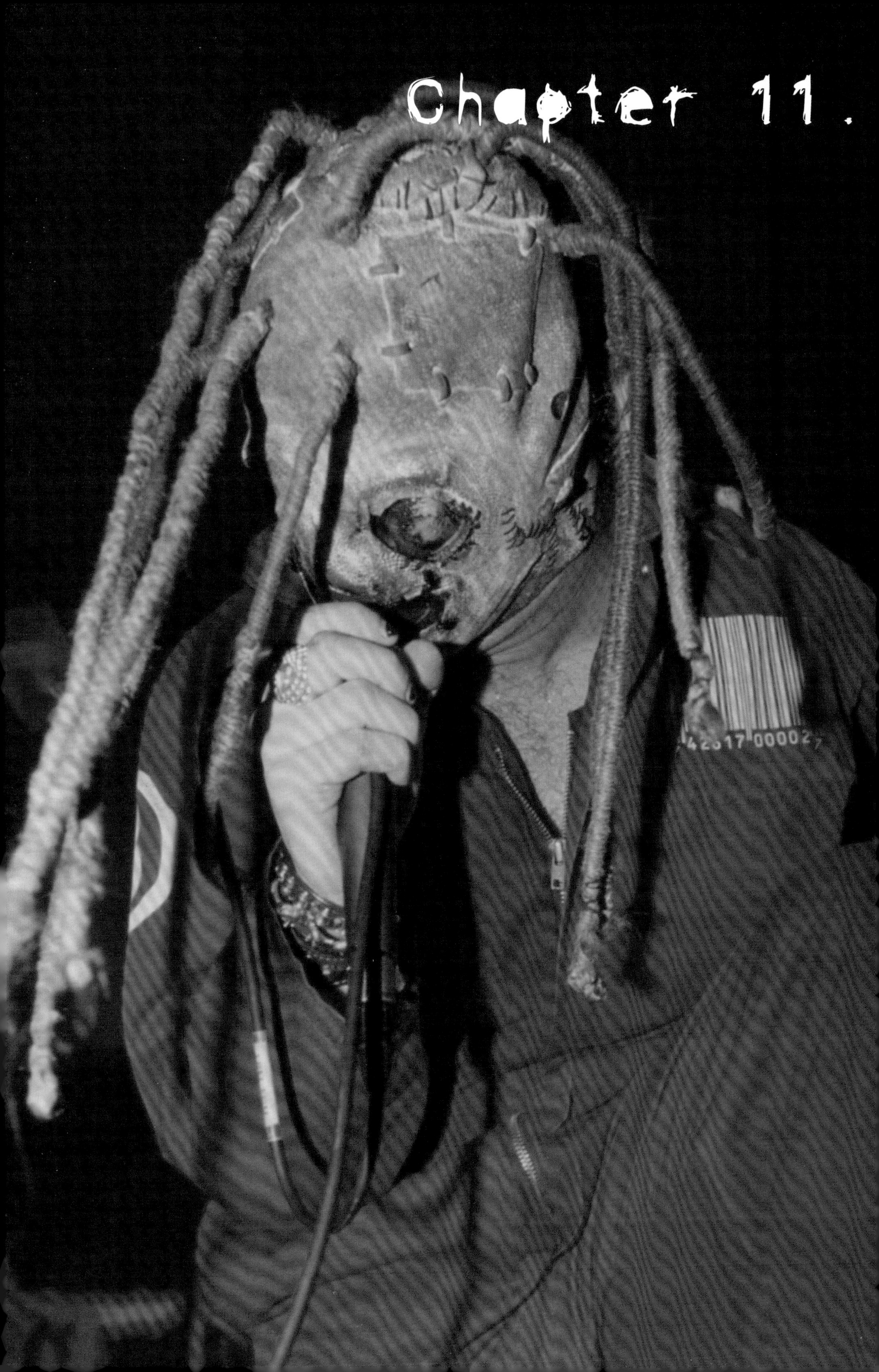

Fighting Talk

With all the anger bundled up in their music, it is perhaps not surprising that Slipknot have ruffled a few feathers and trod on a few toes along the way. In accordance with the old maxim, 'Where there's a hit there's a writ', several bands have crawled out of the woodwork claiming that Slipknot have stolen ideas from them. One group in particular, Mushroomhead, have had an ongoing rivalry with Slipknot over their similar use of masks and jump-suits. In addition, a lawsuit has recently been served by another band with the same name, who are claiming prior usage of the Slipknot moniker.

The most celebrated and public run-in the band have encountered to date was with Limp Bizkit frontman Fred Durst. Not best known for his reserve, Durst has also had verbal altercations with Nine Inch Nails' Trent Reznor, Marilyn Manson, Creed and System of a Down. Fred Durst allegedly initiated the war by stating, at the end of 1999, that Slipknot fans were all ugly fat kids. It was also reported that the Limp Bizkit camp had stated that Slipknot wouldn't get anywhere because they were signed to Roadrunner. This left Slipknot fuming, and at a New York show Corey allegedly threatened to kill Fred if he ever bad-mouthed their fans again. In addition to burning his picture on stage, the band took to getting the crowds at gigs to shout 'Fuck Fred Durst' over and over, before they went into the track 'Surfacing'. And, at a record-signing in New York City, Corey wrote 'Fuck Fred' on his hand, which he periodically waived at those present.

The band have also raised the heckles of Green Day. During an instore gig at the Virgin Megastore in London's Oxford Street, Green Day singer Billy Jo Armstrong put on a clown mask that someone threw onto the stage, and proceeded to mock Corey's vocal style. He then threw it off, claiming that Slipknot's masks were ineffective and went on to challenge them to write a good song for a change. Towards the end of the show, Armstrong asked the audience to dedicate the song he was about to sing to the person they most hated in the world and to think about killing them. He suggested they pick someone 'like a Slipknot member'. The increasing profile of 'The Knot' has also brought them to the attention, and subsequently incurred the wrath, of The Insane Clown Posse, who see them as potential rivals. In the ICP song 'Still Stabbin', the band claim that Slipknot wear masks because they were stabbed in the face by the ICP.

Despite these feuds, which have been largely initiated by other bands, it is far from a one-sided tendency and Slipknot started a war all of their own with Korn drummer David Silveria. They were disgusted that Silveria had, in their opinion, fallen into a cliché rock-star trap by posing for a Calvin Klein advertisement. They weren't alone in this condemnation, as the other members of Korn also felt that the adverts were tasteless and didn't suit their image. Slipknot showed their disgust at his actions during a gig in March 2000, at the 9:30 Club in

Washington D.C. In the midst of the show, Paul held up a copy of the magazine *Teen People* in which a version of the offending advert appeared. He then promptly set it alight, after which Shawn stamped on the burning pages.

But it appears that other bands aren't the only ones getting emotional over the Masked Metalmen and both the media and authorities have had their fair share of run-ins with Slipknot. MTV banned the video for the group's debut single *Spit It Out* (Slipknot's live interpretation of the classic horror flick *The Shining*), on the grounds that it was violent, racist, morally subversive and possibly homophobic. So much for artistic expression! Slipknot have also crossed swords with the moral guardians of Ireland's youth. During their 2000 tour they were forced to cancel a gig after the National Parents' Council in Dublin decided that the vulnerable teenagers of the city should not be exposed to what

they considered was an unacceptably depraved show. Although the event organisers cited other reasons for cancelling the near sell-out gig, the moral gate-keepers were jubilant that they may have had a hand in keeping Slipknot out of town.

In another incident, the wearing of creepy customised rubber masks in public led to a potentially dangerous run-in with the police. While en-route to Rolling Stone Records in Norridge, Illinois, the band were putting on their trademark jump-suits and headgear in a parking lot, when local cops caught sight of the group. They thought that the costumed hard rockers were planning to hold up a local jewellery store and ten police cars arrived with guns ready to shoot, forcing the band to the pavement. The confusion was eventually cleared up, and the less than amused officers looked on as the band spent the better part of three hours greeting some 600 fans at the nearby record store.

Chapter 12.

Global Infestation

Throughout 2000, as Slipknot's relentless rollercoasting tour progressed, the band had virtually become media celebrities. This growing profile led to them making an appearance on the CNN show *World Beat* to discuss their views on the MP3 and Napster controversy. The band have proved themselves to be great supporters of the internet and even maintain the two official Slipknot websites themselves. The site www.slipknot1.com is looked after by Craig and his wife, who often answers fans' questions posted on the band's message board under the alias 'KittyMhz'. Shawn and a guitar technician from the band run the second website www.slipknot2.com.

Despite their real commitment to new technologies, the widespread dissemination of their music on the MP3 format has caused them some problems. Their main grumble is that earlier work and rough mixes, that they do not want widely distributed, are now freely available. As an example of this, the band feel that *Mate. Feed. Kill. Repeat.* is not truly representative of the Slipknot sound, especially as only three of the current members, Shawn, Joey and Paul appeared on it. Despite this, tracks from the album are widely available on Napster, and pirated CD-versions can be picked up from the auction site Ebay for a few dollars. Similarly, the band are annoyed that work in progress has been posted on the net. The band recorded a song called 'Snap' at Junior's Motel in Otho, Iowa, that was never meant to be released. Allegedly, someone at Junior's burnt off a copy for themselves and it filtered out onto the World Wide Web.

In addition to the explosion of tracks on the internet, the rock press were now going ballistic over the band. Numerous articles appeared in most major U.S. and European magazines such as *Alternative Press*, *Circus*, *Hit Parader*, *Metal Hammer*, *Metal Maniacs*, *Spin* and *New Metal*. Indeed, *Guitar World* went so far as giving away 3D glasses, allowing readers to have a real-life Slipknot experience without the fear of permanent hearing loss, and the German magazine *Visions* included the *Spit It Out* video on a cover-mount CD sampler. But it was British metal bible *Kerrang!* that rated the masked men of Slipknot most highly, putting them at Number 26 in the magazine's most influential rock bands of all time list. They also published an article on Slayer in which this legendary band talked about how Slipknot had influenced *them* to create a much harder record.

By now, Slipknot infestation had reached a whole new level. After months of relentless touring with virtually no help from mainstream radio or video broadcasters, the Masked Metal Madmen had achieved mega-sales status. On the 9th of May 2000, the band's self-titled debut album was certified platinum by the RIAA, after selling more than 1 million copies in the US. As welcome recognition for their largely unacknowledged hard work on the album, the Slipknot incubation studio, SR Audio, also got a disc to hang on their wall. This accolade was doubly significant for Roadrunner, as it was the first time they had achieved platinum sales with any of their artists. Slipknot was now also beating Korn's current album *Issues* in the weekly charts. Indeed, competition between Korn and Slipknot reached new heights when a member of the 'Kobbers' bad-mouthed Slipknot by saying, "I never heard of such a band!".

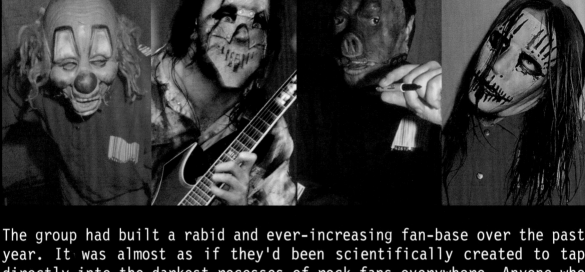

The group had built a rabid and ever-increasing fan-base over the past year. It was almost as if they'd been scientifically created to tap directly into the darkest recesses of rock fans everywhere. Anyone who had caught the group live knew that the emotional give-and-take Slipknot experienced with the audience packed more of a punch than any other rock'n'roll roadshow around. Slipknot's plan had been simple: to infect as many people in the world as possible. The band could even count TV's most connected adolescent, Robert Iler (best known as Anthony Soprano, Jr.), among their most vocal supporters.

On the 29th of August 2000 the Hooded Iowa Rockers walked away from the annual *Kerrang!* Awards at the Hammersmith Palais in London, with three prestigious honours, leaving a path of destruction in their wake. While accepting their first award for Best International Live Act, Sid and Shawn flipped a coin to decide which one would punch the other in the head. Shawn lost and Sid slugged him hard in front of the assembled hoards. The band also picked up Best Single award for 'Wait and Bleed' and the ultimate accolade of Best Band in the World, which they celebrated by back-flipping into the crowd. Bad behaviour from other bands was also widespread and in one notable incident a Cradle of Filth food-fight led to Swedish actress and Rod Stewart's ex-lover, Britt Ekland, slipping on a piece of melon and breaking her ankle. To keep the side up, Slipknot threw glasses on the stage and even found time to set fire to their table, before smashing it to pieces and throwing the detritus at nearby attendees.

In September 2000, Slipknot were set to return to the record racks with the release of a numbered, limited edition, vinyl picture-disc version of their self-titled album. In addition, they also re-issued *Slipknot* as a CD Digipack which boasted an extra six tracks of live recordings, remixes and B-sides, all previously unavailable or hard to find elsewhere. Slipknot were now poised for a headlining fall tour across the US, but the relentless gigging and promotion again took its toll. After a member of the band passed out while at LAX airport in Los Angeles, Slipknot decided, on the 15th of September, to cancel the tour alto-

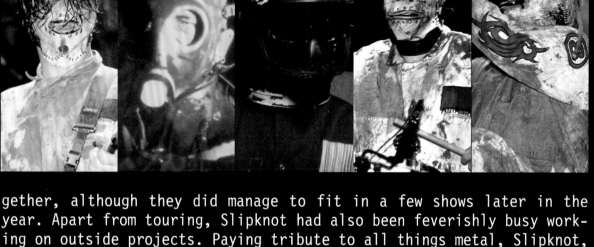

gether, although they did manage to fit in a few shows later in the year. Apart from touring, Slipknot had also been feverishly busy working on outside projects. Paying tribute to all things metal, Slipknot, along with the likes of Lit, Sevendust, Kittie and Type O Negative had earlier in the year put their names forward for an upcoming tribute album saluting 80's glam-rockers Twisted Sister. The band had eagerly expressed an interest in revisiting this virtually forgotten group's catalogue.

Certain 'Knot members had also become wanted commodities. While tub-thumper Shawn Crahan was featured as executive producer on a Mudvayne album, Slipknotter Corey Taylor got together with fellow heavy music purveyors Soulfly. After much planning and schedule shuffling, the Slipknot frontman joined them in the studio to record a track, 'Jumpdafuckup', for the Brazilian band's new album *Primitive*. Slipknot and Soulfly had been trying to make an in-the-studio pairing happen for weeks, and finally found the opportunity when Slipknot's tour rolled into Phoenix, Arizona, where Soulfly were by chance recording. In October 2000, Taylor also contributed a new song entitled 'Requiem' for an Immortal Records CD tribute to the late James Lynn Strait, formerly of Snot. The subsequent album *Strait Up* also contained tracks by members of Soulfly, Coal Chamber, System of a Down, Korn, Limp Bizkit, Sevendust and (hed) pe.

so far is just foreplay. Part of their future master plan for world domination is the release of the follow-up album to their major label debut. On the 11th of January 2001, Slipknot left Des Moines for Sound City Studios in Los Angeles to make a start on the new record. With Ross Robinson in the production hot seat once again, the group were certainly not planning to rehash their earlier work. Keen to move their style forward and to avoid stagnation, the new tracks were going to be harder, sicker, faster and more technical than anything they'd previously recorded. Provisional cuts for the album included the song 'People=Shit' and a cover of The Terriorzers' 'Fear Napalm'. Slipknot have confirmed that they will change masks in time for the release of the album, which is set for Summer 2001. Whatever the final content, we can be assured that this new offering will prove once and for all that Slipknot are not one-hit wonders.

The members are also currently involved in several other side-projects. In early 2001, Corey was back at SR Audio working with old producer Sean McMahon on the mysteriously titled Project X. Amongst others, this includes ex-Slipknot vocalist Anders Colsefni as well as Josh Rand, Shawn Crahan, Sa-Tone (Shawn's drum tech) and Shawn's son Gage. The projected album, which is provisionally entitled *Superego: Click Here To Enter*, is due to be released in mid-2001. Sid Wilson is currently recording under the pseudonym DJ Starscream, and is set to release a solo debut effort on 1500 Records later in the year.

Joey Jordison is recording as guitarist for his other band The Rejects, and is working on a grindcore death metal album with bass guitarist Danny Lilker from Stormtroopers Of Death. This busy guy is also putting a project together with System Of A Down guitarist Daron Malakian and Mudvayne bassist Ryan Martinie. If that was not enough to keep him occupied, in January 2001 he remixed Marilyn Manson's 'The Fight Song' with producer Sean McMahon at SR Audio. This track was the latest single release from Manson's *Holy Wood* album, and Joey's work, which involved adding drum parts, samples and effects, can be heard on the B side.

In the midst of recording their new album and working on various solo projects, it was confirmed in late January 2001 that *Slipknot* had gone Platinum in Australia. With similar awards for record sales in the USA and Europe the previous year, Slipknot were now a truly global phenomenon. In acknowledgement of the quality of their work, they've achieved a Grammy nomination for Best Metal Performance, with the

Deftones, Iron Maiden, Marilyn Manson and Pantera also shortlisted. To top off a bumper twelve-months, Slipknot were declared People of the Year in the December 2000 issue of *Rolling Stone* magazine.

With massive album sales, a host of media accolades and sell-out tours, the band could be forgiven for allowing this success to go to their

upper regions. But that just ain't their style. Although they're understandably ecstatic about their achievements and love their work, when the show's over, they wind their way back to good ol' Des Moines. Once there, the band claim to find it easy to return to their old routines, hang out in the familiar bars and music venues and catch up with friends. The local music scene in Des Moines has received a lot more attention from outside thanks to Slipknot's success. As a result of this, other Des Moines bands such as 35" Mudder and Mr. Plow have been hotly tipped for success and are both currently negotiating deals of their own. It may seem perverse after dreaming of escaping their hometown for so many years, but Slipknot steadfastly refuse to sell up and move out to LA. Des Moines is their home and, for better or worse, that is where they are going to stay. But as much as they value hanging out at home, the band are keen to launch a further tour in Europe and Australia during 2001. Provisionally titled the People=Shit Tour, it is planned to accompany the release of the new album. Mooted opening bands include Mudvayne, Amen, Downset and Coal Chamber.

From this present transitional viewpoint, Slipknot have already come a long way. What began as a side project for a bunch of suppressed headbangers has mutated into a nine-member metal monstrosity. Even if they all packed it in tomorrow, they have already changed the world for devoted fans, providing an outlet that was previously missing in their lives. Indeed, Slipknot would probably be the first to admit that they are just a bunch of rock'n'roll geeks who speak to fans in a language that they understand, because they're just like them. Such is the unbridled intensity that each and every one of them feel for the band, that the members of Slipknot regard themselves as their own biggest fans.

If off-the-wall experience and abnormality are what you search for, search no more. Because Des Moines' mobsters Slipknot will take you there. Misfits... maybe. Weirdoes... possibly. Freaks... definitely.

Lucifer's children... who's to say? Call them what you will, Slipknot don't really give a damn. They know who they are, they do what they want for themselves, and they get off on it. Without a single recognisable face in the group, they crawl their way into your consciousness and stay there, laughing at you in the mist as you frantically try to identify the source of your inner fears. Slipknot is the throb in your pulsating hangover as well as the empty paracetamol bottle you grasp for relief. Slipknot is the disease for which there is no cure. Nine black-hearted psychopaths with thousand-yard, serial killer stares. Slipknot are here to truly dirty up your minds.

These intense, focussed individuals have the worst attitude in the world. With a psychotic-induced energy, they claim to hate everyone and everything, and they will stop at nothing to deliver a humungous 'fuck you' to all detractors. Put simply, they have a fire in their bellies that refuses to go out. So stand aside Marilyn Manson, roll over Metallica and tell Korn the news - Masked Madmen Slipknot are using leather bondage hoods, spiked divers' helmets and drum kits made from outer space debris. Now the world has no choice. Slipknot have arrived and laid down the gauntlet. The metal scene has changed dramatically over the last couple of years. During this time a kind of preparation has been inflicted on the world in order that its new masters might have a ready platform. Like Elvis with rock and roll, The Beatles with pop and Nirvana with grunge, the true masters of nu-metal have arrived.

They are Slipknot. Be afraid. Be very afraid.

Chapter 14.
Slipknot
family tree

Heads On The Wall
(1989)
Shawn Crahan's late-80's
High-School band.
Played locally.

Anal Blast
(1994)
Grindcore band with 25-stone Don Decker
on vocals. Gross stage act included
pulling tampons from his butt and
throwing them into the crowd.
Don Decker — Vocals
Paul Gray — Bass
Joey Jordison — Drums
Donnie Steele — Guitar

Slipknot: Version 1
(1995-1996)
Line-up for 'demo' album *Mate. Feed. Kill. Repea*
Anders Colsefni — Vocals
Paul Gray — Bass/Backing Vocals
Shawn Crahan — Percussion/Backing Vocals
Donnie Steele — Guitar
Josh Brainard — Guitars/Backing Vocals
Joey Jordison — Drums

Stone Sour
(1993-1997)
Corey Taylor's alternative rock
group that Slipknot beat in the
Battle of Bands competition. Corey
later joined Slipknot and several
ex-Stone Sour members are now roadies
and technicians in the Slipknot crew.

Slipknot: Version 5
(1999-Present Day)
Corey Taylor — Vocals
Paul Gray — Bass/Backing Vocals
Shawn Crahan — Percussion/Backing Vocals
Chris Fehn — Percussion
Craig Jones — Guitar
Mick Thompson — Guitar
James Root — Guitars/Backing Vocals
Joey Jordison — Drums

VeXX
(1989-91)

Inveigh Catharsis
(1991-93)

Anders Colsefni's High-School band.
Played covers ranging from Kiss to Slayer,
performing at school and local venues.
Josh Brainard – Guitar and Vocals
Paul Gray – Bass
Anders Colsefni – Drums

Atomic Opera
(1990-93)

hrash-metal/funk-metal trio
hat toured through Iowa and
featured future Slipknotter
Josh Brainard on guitar.

Modifidious
(1993-95)

Speed-metal/thrash band.
Josh Brainard – Vocals & Guitar
Joey Jordison – Drums
Craig Jones – Guitar

Body Pit
(1993-95)

Death-metal band.
Mick Thompson – Guitar
Donnie Steele – Guitar
Danny Spain – Drums
Paul Gray – Bass
Anders Colsefni – Vocals

Slipknot: Version 2
(1996-Late 1997)

Anders Colsefni – Vocals
Paul Gray – Bass/Backing Vocals
Shawn Crahan – Percussion/Backing Vocals
Craig Jones – Guitar
Mick Thompson – Guitar
Josh Brainard – Guitars/Backing Vocal
Joey Jordison – Drums

Slipknot: Version 3
(Late 1997-September 1998)

Corey Taylor – Vocals
Paul Gray – Bass/Backing Vocals
Shawn Crahan – Percussion/Backing Vocals
Greg Welts (Cuddles) – Percussion
Craig Jones – Guitar
Mick Thompson – Guitar
Josh Brainard – Guitars/Backing Vocals
Joey Jordison – Drums

Slipknot: Version 4
(September 1998 - Early 1999)

Line-up that recorded Slipknot.
Corey Taylor – Vocals
Paul Gray – Bass/Backing Vocals
Shawn Crahan – Percussion/Backing Vocals
Chris Fehn – Percussion
Craig Jones – Guitar
Mick Thompson – Guitar
Josh Brainard – Guitars/Backing Vocals
Joey Jordison – Drums

Painface
(1997-Present Day)

Anders' post-Slipknot band
with fellow ex-Body Pit
member Danny Spain on
drums. Death-metal style.

75

Chapter 15

Number: 0

Name: Sid Wilson.
Nickname: 'Ratboy' because of his hair and 'Monkeyboy' for his acrobatic skills.
Instrument: Turntables.
Age: At 22, Sid is the youngest member of Slipknot.
Marital Status: Single.
Previous Jobs:
DJ at raves in Des Moines.
Other Bands: Currently part of a DJ-group called SPC (The Soundproof Coalition).
Mask: Striking black gas mask. Sid has eight different versions in his collection, all with different names. On occasion, they have been known to give him 'organic brain syndrome' as they prevent oxygen from entering his body and cause him to have hallucinations and nausea.
Profile: Sid can be heard providing the scratching behind Slipknot's music. He is the dedicated crowd-surfer of the band and loves nothing better than fighting with number 6.

Number: 1

Name: Nathan Jonas Jordison, or Joey to his friends.
Nickname: 'Superball' which came about following a rare bad performance by the band which made him so mad he bounced around the room to express his annoyance.
Instrument: Drums.
Age: 24.
Marital Status: Single.
Previous Jobs: In the past, Joey has worked in a record store and at a Des Moines gas station.
Other Bands: Before Slipknot, Joey was in the bands Modifidious, with Josh and Craig, and Anal Blast with Paul and ex-Slipknot guitarist Donnie.
Mask: Joey sports an expressionless, oriental-style Kabuki mask with scars painted across its forehead and mouth. His wearing of this particular face covering was actually inspired by his mother! After a night out, Joey returned home late to find his mother hiding behind the door with the mask and a robe on. Needless to say, it scared the living daylights out of him, an experience he remembers all to well to this day.
Profile: Joey is generally thought to be one of the best drummers around and writes much of Slipknot's music and lyrics. In addition, his mixing skills were used to great effect on *Mate. Feed. Kill. Repeat.* To help his movement while drumming, he cuts off the sleeves and legs of his Slipknot outfit so he can move more freely.

Number: 2

Name: Paul Gray.
Nickname: 'Balls' on account
of his fearless nature.
Instrument: Bass Guitar.
Age: 27.
Marital Status: Single.
Previous Jobs: Construction worker.
Other Bands: Prior to joining
Slipknot, Paul was in the band VeXX
with Josh and ex-Slipknot vocalist
Anders. He also played with Joey and
ex-Slipknot guitarist Donnie in the band Anal Blast,
and with Mick, Donnie and Anders in the group Body Pit.
Mask: Open-mouthed pig mask with pierced septum.
Profile: Paul, the quiet member of the group is the only Slipknotter
who is not a true Des Moines native. He was born in Los Angeles
but moved to Slipknot's hometown when he was a teenager.

Number: 3

Name: Chris Fehn.
Nickname: 'Bud' on account of him
always saying 'what's up Bud?' and
'Mr Picklenose' because of the
Pinocchio protrusion on his mask.
Instrument: Percussion and
backing vocals.
Age: 27.
Marital Status: Single.
Previous Jobs: Burger King.
Other Bands: None.
Mask: Wears a bondage/fetish-type mask attached to a leather hood with kinky
zip-up lips and an appropriately sized nose (some 7-8 inches long) to boot.
Profile: The joker in the pack, Chris has the bizarre habit of 'jacking' off
his nose from time to time, something which he even did on US Network television!
Chris is a dedicated sports fanatic and rather handy golfer.

Number: 4

Name: James Root.
Nickname: 'The Peach'. This curious
nickname is a reference to the Roald
Dahl book 'James and the Giant Peach'.
Apart from sharing his first name with
the hero of this story, James is also
the tallest in the band and at
6 foot 6 is a real giant.
Instrument: Guitar.
Age: 27.
Marital Status: Single.
Previous Jobs: Washed up dishes in a restaurant.
Other Bands: Before Slipknot, Jim was in the bands Atomic Opera and Dead Front.
Mask: A white-faced court jester's mask with a zipper for a mouth and a spike on the
chin. Over time, Jim has sweated, snotted and puked in it to such an extent that
it is now really disgusting and stinks out everywhere he leaves it.
Profile: Joined the band as replacement for Josh. When he signed up, Jim took to wear-
ing Josh's bondage hood, but this caused him some serious problems. Not only was it excruciat-
ingly painful, but it also used to fill up with so much sweat that he had trouble
hearing. The other band members pressed him to cut holes in the ears to let the per-
spiration out, but after a few gigs he ditched it and developed his own replacement.
Jim also enjoys fishing and playing computer games.

Number: 5

Name: Craig Jones.
Nickname: '133 Mhz' after an old
computer that he used to own.
Instrument: Samplers and keyboards.
Age: 27.
Marital Status: Married.
Previous Jobs: Paper Round.
Other Bands: Craig also played in
the band Modifidious with Josh and
Joey before they joined Slipknot.

Mask: Onstage, Craig wears an ex-Sinclair gas station racing helmet
with a crown of spikes poking out of the top. These spikes are made
out of real nine-inch nails that he fixed himself.
Profile: The Slipknot sampling mix-master started off duties in the band as a
guitarist, but soon began handling all the samples for the band, making
their songs sound as freaky and eerie as possible. A total computer game fan, Craig
jealously guards his anonymity to such an extent that he refuses to play an active
role in press conferences, even covering his eyes with leather patches. See above!

Number: 6

Name: Shawn Crahan.
Nickname: 'The Clown' on account
of his mask and 'Kong'
because of his body size.
Instrument: Percussion including
titanium drums, kegs and barrels.
Age: At 30 years of age, Shawn is
the oldest member of the group.
Marital Status: Married to Chantal with
three kids (two girls and a boy).
Previous Jobs: Worked in real estate
and was a welder.
Other Bands: Heads on the Wall.

Mask: A plain old customised clown mask made of rubber which he nicknames 'Dude'.
Profile: Shawn is the founder of the group and the real business-minded member who,
along with Paul, takes the role of spokesman. During shows Shawn likes to start all
sorts of fights on stage (usually with DJ Sid) and ends up trashing most of the
band's equipment. However, his experience in all things metallic, especially welding,
have been put to good use. Shawn builds much of Slipknot's stage props, including a
wacky drum-riser on springs. He also designed the world's first titanium drums,
which he has custom-made to be virtually indestructible.

Number: 7

Name: Mick Thompson.
Nickname: 'Log' on account of him being
6 foot 2 and having a huge body frame.
Instrument: Guitar.
Age: 26.
Marital Status: Single.
Previous Jobs: Guitar tutor at
Ye Olde Guitar Shop in Des Moines.
Other Bands: Before becoming Slipknot's
guitarist, Mick was in the band
Body Pit with Paul and ex-Slipknot
members Anders, Danny and Donnie.

Mask: Mean-looking metal ice-hockey mask.
Profile: Mick is a real paradox. Although he has an obsession with serial killers,
he also loves cats and is an avid fisherman. Despite this, no one messes with
him on stage, not even Shawn.

Number: 8

Name: Corey Taylor
Nickname: 'The Sickness' because of his disturbing fantasies and 'Faith' because of his dedication to the church of Slipknot.
Instrument: Vocals.
Age: 26.
Marital Status: Recently engaged.
Previous Jobs: Corey had an illustrious former career working for three years at a porno book shop called The Adult Emporium. He has been a great porn-aficionado since the age of 13, and thought that all his Christmases had come at once when a friend actually got him a job peddling 'the filth' he loved. Corey used to work the night shift from midnight to eight, a time that gave him space to think and inspired a lot of his later lyrics.
Other Bands: Before Slipknot, Corey was in the band Stone Sour.
Mask: Wears a pale leather facemask that sprouts an array of brown and blonde dreadlocks. In the past, he used to poke his own hair through the holes on the top before every gig, but this used to cause him a substantial amount of pain. As a result, he decided to cut off some of his hair and sew it onto the mask to save him the trouble.
Profile: Corey also has a huge collection of action figures that he has been accumulating since he was a kid, and is a big fan of comic books. He loves nothing better than a good movie and not surprisingly his favourite film is The Texas Chainsaw Massacre. He also has the Japanese character for death tattooed on one side of his neck, and the character for father on the other, in his case a man he never knew.

Chapter 16

Slipknot
LIBERATING MANCHESTER

Slipknot

Slipknot
wait and bleed

Slipknot
MASSAKER

Live in London '99

discography

ALBUMS:

Mate. Feed. Kill. Repeat.: *Slipknot / Gently / Do Nothing/Bitch Slap / Only One / Tattered And Torn / Confessions / Some Feel / Killers Are Quiet* - Slipknot's self-funded demo release, limited to 1000 copies and no longer available.
CD - 1996

Slipknot: *742617000027 / (Sic) / Eyeless / Wait And Bleed / Surfacing / Spit It Out / Tattered And Torn / Frail Limb Nursery / Purity / Liberate / Prosthetics / No Life / Diluted / Only One / Scissors / Eeyore (Hidden Track)* - This is the original version which was released on June 19th 1999. Due to legal problems involving www.crimescene.com as outlined in the text, the songs *Frail Limb Nursery* and *Purity* were removed and replaced by *Me Inside*. This album has been released with numerous different track listings, the main ones you will find are listed below.
CD, LP and Cassette — Roadrunner 1999

Slipknot: *742617000027 / (Sic) / Eyeless / Wait And Bleed / Surfacing / Spit It Out / Tattered And Torn / Me Inside / Liberate / Prosthetics / No Life / Diluted / Only One / Scissors*
CD, LP and Cassette — Roadrunner 1999

Slipknot: *742617000027 / (Sic) / Eyeless / Wait And Bleed / Surfacing / Spit It Out / Tattered And Torn / Liberate / Prosthetics / No Life / Diluted / Only One / Scissors / Me Inside (Bonus Track) / Get This (Bonus Track) / Interloper (Demo Bonus Track) / Despise (Demo Bonus Track)*
CD Digipack, limited edition with four bonus tracks - Roadrunner 1999

Slipknot: *742617000027 / (Sic) / Eyeless / Wait And Bleed / Surfacing / Spit It Out / Tattered And Torn / Me Inside / Liberate / Prosthetics / No Life / Diluted / Only One / Scissors*
LP, limited edition green vinyl — Roadrunner 2000

Slipknot: *742617000027 / (Sic) / Eyeless / Wait And Bleed / Surfacing / Spit It Out / Tattered And Torn / Me Inside / Liberate / Prosthetics / No Life / Diluted / Only One / Scissors / Get This (Bonus Track) / Spit It Out (Hyper Version Bonus Track) / Wait And Bleed (Terry Date Re-mixed Bonus Track) / Interloper (Demo Bonus Track) / Despise (Demo Bonus Track) / Surfacing (Live Bonus Track)*
CD Digipack with six bonus tracks — Roadrunner 2000

Slipknot: *742617000027 / (Sic) / Eyeless / Wait And Bleed / Surfacing / Spit It Out / Tattered And Torn / Me Inside / Liberate / Prosthetics / No Life / Diluted / Only One / Scissors / Get This / Interloper (Demo Bonus Track) / Despise (Demo Bonus Track)*
CD, Japanese limited edition - Roadrunner 2000

Slipknot: *742617000027 / (Sic) / Eyeless / Wait And Bleed / Surfacing / Spit It Out / Tattered And Torn / Me Inside / Liberate / Prosthetics / No Life / Diluted / Only One / Scissors*
LP, limited edition picture disc — Roadrunner 2000

Slipknot: *742617000027 / (Sic) / Eyeless / Wait And Bleed / Surfacing (Rough Mix) / Spit It Out / Tattered And Torn / Me Inside / Liberate / Prosthetics / No Life / Diluted / Only One / Scissors / Eeyore (Hidden Bonus Track)*
CD, European limited edition with two bonus tracks - Roadrunner 2000

SINGLES:

Spit It Out: *Spit It Out / Surfacing (Live)*
7-inch single, red vinyl - Roadrunner 2000

Spit It Out: *Spit It Out / Surfacing (Live) / Wait And Bleed (Live)*
CD single, enhanced version - Roadrunner 2000

Spit It Out: *Spit It Out / Surfacing (Live) / Wait And Bleed (Live) / Spit It Out (CD-Rom Video)*
CD single, enhanced version - Roadrunner 2000

Wait & Bleed: *Wait And Bleed (Terry Date Mix) / Spit It Out (Overcaffeinated Hyper Version) / (Sic)(Molt Injected Mix)*
12-inch single - Roadrunner 2000

Wait & Bleed: *Wait And Bleed (Terry Date Mix) / Spit It Out (Overcaffeinated Hyper Version) / (Sic)(Molt Injected Mix) / Enhanced Video*
CD single - Roadrunner 2000

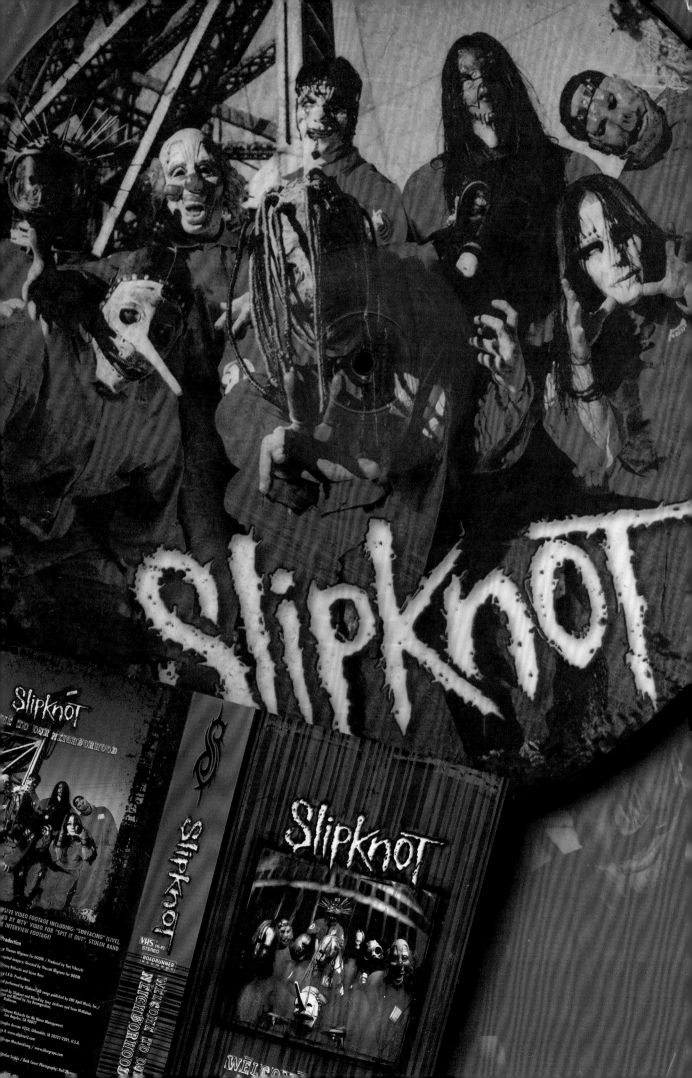

Maggot Corps: *Spit It Out (Single Version) / Surfacing (Live) / Wait And Bleed (Live) / Spit It Out (Enhanced Video) / Wait And Bleed (Terry Date Mix) / Spit It Out (Overcaffeinated Hyper Version) / Sic (Molt Injected Mix) / Wait And Bleed (Enhanced Video)/ Interviews With Band Members* - 3 CD Singles housed in a box with Official Maggot Corps sticker, Official Maggot Corps patch and a black T-shirt with two-color Maggot Corps design.
CD single collection - Pap 2000

COMPILATIONS:

The Hard and The Heavy: *Spit It Out*
CD — Redline Records 1999

Free Air Volume 2 — Music for Motorcross: *Wait And Bleed*
CD - Go Big Records 2000

Tattoo The Earth - The First Crusade Live (Various Artists): *Liberate / Surfacing*
CD - 1500 Records/Red 2000

Tattoo The Earth - The First Crusade Live (Various Artists): *Liberate / Surfacing / Spit It Out*
CD - edited version - 1500 Records/Red 2000

MTV's Return of the Rock, Volume 1: *Spit It Out*
CD — Roadrunner 2000

Scream 3 Soundtrack: *Wait And Bleed*
CD - BMG/Wind Up 2000

Download 2: *Surfacing (Rough Mix)*
CD — Sored 2000

Ozzfest '99 'We sold our soul for rock and roll!': *Surfacing / Eyeless*
- live recordings from the Ozzfest 1999 summer festival.
CD — Roadrunner 2000

Kerrang's 'Spirit of Independence': *Eyeless*
CD — Kerrang! 2000

Sweating Bullets: *Wait and Bleed*
CD — Castle 2000

COLLABORATIONS WITH OTHERS:

Primitive: *Jumpdafuckup* Soulfly - collaboration with Corey Taylor.
CD – Roadrunner 2000

Strait Up: *Requiem* - Corey Taylor performs on track for tribute album to the late Snot band member Lyn Strait. Also includes tracks featuring Jonathan Davis of Korn, Dez Fafara of Coal Chamber, Max Cavalera of Soulfly and many more.
CD - EMD/Virgin 2000

BOOTLEGS:

Bootlegs are unofficial releases of mixes, live recordings, downloads and rare tracks. There are numerous CDs around featuring Slipknot, and below is a selection of the most common ones. It should be noted that to sell or trade in bootleg material is a criminal offence, therefore they are only available from underground sources such as market stalls and record fairs. The authors and publishers of the book do not endorse any trade in such items nor do they have any further information about their availability.

Slipknot at Ozzfest '99: *(Sic) / Eyeless / Liberate / Surfacing / Purity / Spit It Out / Wait And Bleed / Eeyore*
CD

Live in Manchester UK: *(Sic) / Eyeless / Wait And Bleed / Liberate / Surfacing / Purity / Spit It Out / Only One / Get This / Scissors*
CD

Liberating Manchester: *742617000027 / (Sic) / Eyeless / Wait And Bleed / Liberate / Surfacing / Purity / Spit It Out / Only One / Get This / Scissors / Wait And Bleed / Interloper (Demo) / Despise (Demo)* - Tracks 1 to 11 recorded live at Manchester Academy, 19th February 2000. Track 12 taken from TFI Friday appearance, 3rd March 2000. Tracks 13 and 14 are demos.
CD

Live in Melbourne: *Rabbit Intro / 742617000027 / (Sic) / Eyeless / Wait And Bleed / Liberate / Surfacing / Purity / Me Inside / Spit It Out / Get This / Scissors / My Mistake* - Concert recorded at the Royal Festival Hall, Melbourne.
CD

Live in San Brendino, Ozzfest 1999: *Intro / (Sic) / Eyeless / Wait And Bleed / Surfacing / Purity / Spit It Out*
CD

Live In Stockholm: *742617000027 / (Sic) / Eyeless / Wait And Bleed / Liberate / Surfacing / Purity / Prosthetics / Spit It Out / Get This / Scissors / Outro*
CD

Live in Toronto: *Intro / (Sic) / Eyeless / Wait And Bleed / No Life / Liberate / Purity / Prosthetics / Spit It Out / Eeyore / Surfacing / Scissors* - Concert recorded at The Warehouse in Toronto.
CD

London=Shit: *Intro / 742617000027 / (Sic) / Eyeless / Wait And Bleed / Liberate / Surfacing / Purity / Prosthetics / Spit It Out / Eeyore / Scissors*
CD

Live In London '99: *Intro / 742617000027 / (Sic) / Eyeless / Wait And Bleed / Liberate / Surfacing / Despise / Prosthetics / Spit It Out /Eeyore / Scissors* - Tracks recorded during performance in London, 13th December 1999.
CD

Massaker: *Slipknot / Gently / Do Nothing/Bitch Slap / Only One / Tattered And Torn / Confessions / Some Feel / Killers Are Quiet / Eeyore / (sic) / Eyeless / Wait And Bleed / Liberate / Surfacing / Purity / Spit It Out / Only One / Get This* - Tracks 1 to 8 are from **Mate. Feed. Kill. Repeat.** while tracks 10 to 18 were recorded during a live show at the Manchester Academy.
CD

Mate. Feed. Kill. Repeat.: *Slipknot / Gently / Do Nothing/Bitch Slap / Only One / Tattered And Torn / Confessions / Some Feel / Killers Are Quiet / Eyeless (Rough Mix) / Surfacing (Rough Mix) / Me Inside / Get This / Spit It Out (Rough Mix) / Interloper (Demo) / Despise (Demo)* - Tracks 1 to 8 are from **Mate. Feed. Kill. Repeat.** while tracks 9 to 15 are various bonus tracks.
CD

Winipeg 1998: *742617000027 / (Sic) / Eyeless / Wait And Bleed / Surfacing / Purity / Spit It Out / Eeyore / Scissors*
CD

BOOKS AND AUDIO BOOKS:

Maximum Slipknot - Audio Biography with interviews and free mini-poster.
CD - Chrome Dreams 2000

Barcode Killers: *The Slipknot Story in Words and Pictures*
Chrome Dreams 2001

VIDEOS:

Slipknot: Welcome to Our Neighbourhood - Limited edition, behind the scenes 20-minute 'home-video' biography. Features videos of *Surfacing (Live Ozzfest 1999 recording), Spit It Out, Wait And Bleed (Live Ozzfest 1999 recording), (Sic) (Home footage), Interview clips with band*
VHS - Director Thomas Mignone — Roadrunner 1999

Loud Times Video Magazine Issue #3 - Interview with Slipknot's Chris and Corey.
VHS - Loud Times 2000

WEBSITES:

For sourcing additional information about Slipknot, you really can't beat the World Wide Web. There are literally hundreds of Slipknot sites that contain a wide range of biographical information, pictures, up-to-the-minute news and tour dates as well as MP3's of both their well known and rarer tracks. The following sites are among the most comprehensive and a good place to start finding out about Slipknot online.

www.slipknot1.com - Official band website.
www.slipknot2.com - Official band website.
www.slipknotweb.com
www.slipknotband.homestead.com
www.crowz.org
www.mfkr1.com
www.sraudio.com - Home of Slipknot, where **Mate. Feed. Kill. Repeat.** was recorded and the band still record various solo projects.
www.roadrunnerrecords.com - Slipknot's record label.
www.slipknotband.com - Slipknot message board.

17.

photos courtesy of:

REDFERNS LONDON
PICTORIAL PRESS LONDON
FAMOUS LONDON
ALL ACTION LONDON
STAR FILE PHOTO NEW YORK
MIKE LAWYER AT SR AUDIO

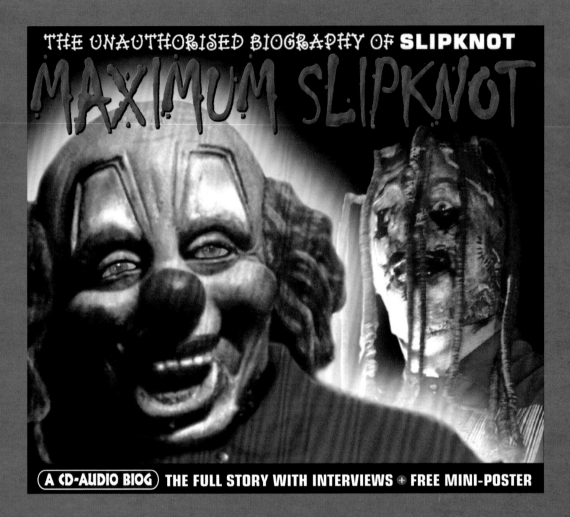